The Upper Room Ministry
of the Lord Jesus

by

Albert Leckie

The Upper Room Ministry of the Lord Jesus

by

Albert Leckie

Precious Seed Publications

ISBN: 978-1-913113-02-5

Printed in the UK

Preface

A few words regarding the fact that this book is being published more than thirty years after Albert Leckie was called home to be with the Lord might help the reader to appreciate its contents and format.

For nearly thirty years Mr. Leckie conducted the Trimsaran Bible Readings in south-west Wales. These were held in August each year and proved to be helpful to many believers in their understanding of a wide range of truth. From 1977-79 the Readings were devoted to the study of John chapters 13 to 17. These have been transcribed and edited into a form suitable for publication and this book is the result.

Mr. Leckie delighted in the truth conveyed by our Lord in the upper room and his clear expositional and practical teaching will afford real help to the reader. This book contains many glorious themes of truth in respect of the person and work of both our Lord Jesus Christ and the Holy Spirit, and the fellowship with divine persons that is enjoyed by the children of God. The book will remind an older generation of the rich ministry enjoyed from our brother and establish younger believers in the faith once for all delivered to us. Because of the way the book has been prepared it has not been possible to include any bibliography or references. It is unlikely that everything in this book is original, but the reader will discover delightful lines of truth not commonly expressed elsewhere.

Strenuous efforts have been made to discover the whereabouts of our brother's notes, particularly those bound in Oxford Loose Leaf Bible covers, but they have not been successful. A further plea is made that if their whereabouts are known they be made available to assist in future publications.

The publishers are grateful to John Stock for making available recordings of the Bible Readings and to Gary Williamson, Sheila Giraldi, Sherry Teo, Joelle Cowie and Andrea Glenny for valued assistance in transcribing the original recordings.

This is the fourth book in this series, following on from *Romans 1-8*, *The Tabernacle and The Offerings* and *1 John*. May the Lord be pleased to use it to the blessing of the Lord's people, that there might be a deeper understanding of our Saviour's person and work and a greater devotion to Him.

Ian Jackson
Eastbourne
January, 2020

Contents

Chapter 13

There are three main sections in this chapter.

In verses 1 to 20 there is the action parable given by the Lord Jesus in the matter of washing and wiping His disciples' feet. Then, in verses 21 to 30, there is the self-excommunication of Judas the traitor who 'went . . . out: and it was night', v. 30. Finally, in verses 31 to 38, the Lord announces to His disciples His departure, 'yet a little while I am with you', v. 33.

There is another delightful connection in these sections. In verses 1 to 5, there is **love assured**, 'having loved his own which were in the world, he loved them unto the end', v. 1. In verses 6 to 11, there is **communion desired**. In verse 8, the Lord says, 'If I wash thee not, thou hast no part with me'. Then, in verses 12 to 17, there is **submission expected**. He says in verse 14, 'If I then, your Lord and Master, have washed your feet; ye also ought to wash one another's feet'. Then, in verses 18 to 20, there is **faith strengthened**. He says in verse 19, 'Now I tell you before it come, that, when it is come to pass, ye may believe that I am'. He tells them that their faith will be strengthened in the fact that He is the great I am of eternity.

The **setting** of the chapter is very important. There are two key verses in John chapter 13. In verse 1, we are told that 'Jesus knew that his hour was come that he should depart out of this world unto the Father'. Then, in verse 3, He knew that 'he was come from God, and went to God'. In this chapter, therefore, the Son of God is standing on the very eve of His departure from this world, knowing that He is going back to the Father and that He is going back to God. It would appear that the very glory of heaven is calling Him back and He is aware that there is awaiting Him not only the Father's throne but also the Father's welcome.

Though He knew this He still had an interest here on the earth, 'his own which were in the world', v. 1. As He is about to leave them the heart of the Son of God is overflowing toward them, His desire being that as they were here in this world they might have 'part' with Him, v. 8. He desired that they be in that condition suitable to having communion with Him in the place to which He was going. In order that they might appreciate this, He gives them this action parable in the matter of feet washing.

The **time** of this action parable is important and must be observed. Time terms are brought before us in verse 1, 'before the feast' and in verse 2, 'supper being come', as it should read. The KJV says 'supper being ended' but we know that supper was not, in fact, ended. Some render it, 'supper being laid'. Feet are not washed at the end of supper but at the commencement. The significance of this is that it was the feast of the Passover. No one knew better than the Son of God what that Passover typified and what the fulfilment of the Passover was soon to mean to Him at the place called Calvary. Yet, despite the fact that it was just before the feast, John says in verse 1, 'having loved his own . . . he loved them unto the end'. Everything that was set before them at the supper would make Him think of what He would soon endure on the cross and yet having loved His own He loved them unto the end. Calvary is very near and everything is there to remind Him of it. Then 'He riseth', v. 4, to give expression to the love of His heart.

The **circumstances** of the chapter are to be observed insofar as they relate to the world and to His own. His manifestation to the world is complete, its hatred of Him has been fully exposed and its judgement has been pronounced. He had said, 'Now is the judgment of this world: now shall the prince of this world be cast out', 12. 31. Jerusalem's verdict with regard to Him was that He was a sinner, 9. 24, that He was mad, 10. 20, that He had a demon, 7. 20; 8. 48, and that He was a blasphemer, 10. 33. Jerusalem's verdict on the Son of God having been reached, His manifestation to the world was now complete.

'His own', on the other hand, were with Him in the upper room. 'His own' is a rather different expression from that which is used in chapter 1 verse 11, where John says, 'He came unto his own [things], and his own [people] received him not'. This is, in chapter 13, a different company, being His apostles. Peter was one of them, whom He found it necessary to rebuke, saying, 'Get thee behind me, Satan: thou art an offence unto me: for thou savourest not the things that be of God, but those that be of men', Matt. 16. 23. This was the same Peter who, before this chapter concludes, was told by the Lord that he would soon deny Him, v. 38. Yet Peter was one of His own.

James and John, too, were part of that company, those sons of thunder whom the Lord found it necessary to rebuke by saying, 'Ye know not what manner of spirit ye are of', Luke 9. 55. Philip also was one of them, to whom the Son of God found it necessary to say in verse 9 of the next chapter, 'Have I been so long time with you, and yet hast thou not known me?'. Indeed, we are told that 'they all forsook him', Mark 14. 50. Soon He was to find Himself in the garden of Gethsemane with all the agony that was there involved. Peter, James and John, the favoured three, would fall asleep there. Each of His own, without exception, failed Him and yet 'he loved them unto the end'.

There are **three main actors** in this action parable, namely Jesus, Peter and Judas Iscariot.

When we think of **Jesus,** there were three things in the opening verses that He knew. Key expressions in John's Gospel are, 'Jesus knew' and 'Jesus knowing': it is the Gospel that speaks of the omniscient Son of God. Here, He knew that He was departing 'out of this world unto the Father', v. 1; that the Father 'had given all things into his hands', v. 3; and 'that He was come from God, and went to God', v. 3. With regard to His disciples, we learn that there was strife amongst them as to which of them should be accounted the greatest, Luke 22. 24, but here God's omniscient Son, in the full consciousness of His own personal dignity and majesty, does the service that was generally undertaken by a slave. As He performs it, He acts wholly by Himself. Angels would gladly have attended and assisted but no one present does so as He girds Himself, taking that basin and that towel, and gets down at the feet of each of His own to wash them and wipe them.

Then there is **Peter**. True to type, Peter both tells the Lord what He is not to do and what He should do. He says in verse 8, 'Thou shalt never wash my feet'. Peter employs the strongest negative in the Greek language, 'Thou shalt never to all eternity' or 'thou shalt never as long as the world lasts' wash my feet. Then, in verse 9, he tells the Lord what

He should do, namely to wash 'not my feet only, but also my hands and my head'.

There is also **Judas Iscariot**. In verses 10 and 11, the Lord Jesus makes it clear that Judas is not clean. Then, in verse 18, it is important to observe that Judas was present with them and that his choice was made that the scripture might be fulfilled. Then, in verses 19 and 20, the Lord Jesus explains to His own in the upper room why it was that at this juncture He had announced the presence of one who would betray Him in their very midst.

There is also the Lord's **lesson on feet-washing** for His disciples. First of all, they submit to His lordship as He washes their feet. Then, as their teacher, He indicates to them the significance of feet-washing.

There is one further important matter that might be profitable to consider in a general way. It was in the upper room on this particular occasion that the Lord Jesus instituted the Lord's Supper, yet, amazingly, John makes no reference to it at all. Matthew was present and, in his Gospel, he gives us his record of the institution of the Lord's Supper. Mark was not present, not being one of the twelve, but, undoubtedly, he received his information from Peter. Luke was not present either, but it is evident that he received his information from Paul, whose constant companion he was, as Luke's record of the institution of the supper is strikingly similar to that of Paul in 1 Corinthians chapter 11. Paul, of course, was not present in the upper room when the supper was instituted but he makes it clear that he received the account of the institution from the Lord Himself, 1 Cor. 11. 23. John, however, was present in the upper room and it was on this occasion that he was leaning on the bosom and lying on the breast of Jesus, vv. 23, 25, yet he makes no mention of the institution of the Lord's Supper.

Though John makes no mention of the bread and the cup, he mentions the basin and the towel. John does not record, as do Luke and Paul, the words of the Lord Jesus, 'this do in remembrance of me', Luke 22. 19; 1 Cor. 11. 24, but he does record how that the Lord Jesus, after He had washed and wiped His disciples' feet, said, 'I have given you an example, that ye should do as I have done to you', v. 15. The basin and the towel are as important as the bread and the cup; and the words of the Lord Jesus, 'I have given you an example, that ye should do as I have done to you' are as important as His words, 'this do in remembrance of me'. John wants to introduce us to the spiritual tone and atmosphere of the upper room when the Lord's supper was instituted, and to direct our attention to conditions that are necessary for the enjoyment of it. After all, the celebration of the Lord's Supper can be meaningless, cold and formal if we do not have the spiritual tone of the upper room. The conditions that are presented to us in feet-washing are necessary for the enjoyment of worship.

The action parable itself, vv. 1-5

In these verses the Lord Jesus is seen as the Son, with His deity being emphasized. He is seen as omniscient and omnipotent. His omniscience is observed in the expressions, 'Jesus knew that his hour was come', v. 1, and 'Jesus knowing that the Father had given all things into his hands', v. 3. His omnipotence is also seen in verse 3, for He has the capacity to receive all things into His hands.

'Now before the feast of the passover, when Jesus knew that his hour was come that he should depart out of this world unto the Father, having loved his own which were in the world, he loved them unto the end', v. 1.

The action parable of the feet washing took place 'before the feast of the passover', when everything was calculated to make our Saviour think of the fulfilment of that feast at the place called Calvary.

In the opening verses there are three things that Jesus knew. In verse 1, He knew 'that his hour was come that he should depart out of this world unto the Father'. Then, in verse 3, there are two further things that He knew: 'that the Father had given all things into his hands' and 'that he was come from God, and went to God'. In verse 11, He 'knew who should betray him'. In the Gospel according to John, key expressions are 'Jesus knew' and 'Jesus knowing'. It is the Gospel that speaks of His omniscience.

13

Some have stumbled at Mark chapter 13, where the Son indicates that He knows not the hour of His coming. There, of course, our Lord Jesus Christ is seen as the servant Son, who deemed it not within His province to think in terms of when He would come again. He left that to His master, for He said, 'The servant knoweth not what his lord doeth', John 15. 15, RV. However, in John's Gospel, the eternal Son of God is seen in all His omniscience and this is a theme which runs throughout the Gospel. It is seen in chapter 1 verse 48 where Jesus says to Nathaniel, 'when thou wast under the fig tree, I saw thee'. In chapter 2, 'Jesus did not commit himself unto them, because he knew all men . . . he knew what was in man', vv. 24, 25. 'Thou hast had five husbands; and he whom thou now hast is not thy husband', is the language of chapter 4 verse 18. In chapter 6 verse 64, 'Jesus knew from the beginning who they were that believed not, and who should betray him'. 'Jesus therefore, knowing all things that should come upon him, went forth', 18. 4. The Gospel concludes with the words of Peter, 'Lord, thou knowest all things; thou knowest that I love thee', 21. 17.

'The hour' is frequently mentioned in John's Gospel. This does not always relate to the same event. For instance, in chapter 2 verse 4, we read, 'Woman, what have I to do with thee? mine hour is not yet come'. He is referring to the hour of His kingdom glory, when He shall change Israel's water into wine. In chapter 7 verse 30, it says, 'his hour was not yet come', referring to His hour of manifestation to the world. Then, 'no man laid hands on him; for his hour was not yet come', 8. 20, the reference being to the hour of His suffering. In this verse, it is the hour of His departing unto the Father, involving the thought of His death, but going beyond that.

The word 'depart' is a different word from the word that Paul uses, for instance, in Philippians chapter 1 verse 23 ('having a desire to depart') or in 2 Timothy chapter 4 verse 6 ('the time of my departure is at hand'). That word, which has to do with the 'taking down' of a body as one would take down a tent, could never be used of the Lord Jesus. Here, 'depart' means 'to be transferred from one scene to another' and does not involve any interruption in being. He was departing out of this world unto the Father. The beauty of scripture, which preserves the uniqueness of the manhood of Christ, may thus be noted.

John speaks frequently of 'this world'. The demonstrative pronoun 'this' emphasizes the present character of this world: it is **this** world, which is not only transient but has its own particular prince, a world system that is away from God.

He knew that He was departing 'unto the Father'. Note that it does not say unto 'His Father' but 'the Father'. He speaks as Son of Man.

'Having loved his own' relates to the 'twelve', technically speaking. Perhaps it might be better to say the eleven, those who were His own. They were His own for a number of reasons and, perhaps, the most important one was that they were those whom the Father had given to Him.

Judas was nominally still one of His own and treated as such until his true character became apparent. In John chapter 6, Jesus knew from the beginning that Judas should betray Him, yet all along He bore with him and treated him as one of His own. The Lord takes up a man on his profession, until it becomes apparent that his profession is unreal.

His own were 'in the world' and He 'loved them unto the end'. The thought in the expression is not one of time, as in 'he that endureth to the end', Matt. 10. 22, where 'the end' is the end of the tribulation period, but it is rather that He loved them with a perfect and a complete love, love to its fullest degree. To introduce the idea of time here hardly fits this section. There is already a time expression, 'before the feast'; if 'unto the end' was an expression of time it would almost seem to mean 'to the end of the feast'.

The love that He exhibited when He laid down His life was no greater than His love for them at any other time. It was always of the highest degree and Calvary would be a manifestation of it. This uttermost of His love is to be seen against the background of His knowledge that He was going to the Father. It might have been thought that with the Son going back to heaven and the Father, all the weariness, work and rejection of this life being over, He would be occupied with the Father's throne and the Father's welcome. However, His thoughts were towards His own whom He loved with the uttermost degree of love.

15

The expression 'the uttermost' in Hebrews chapter 7 verse 25 is a somewhat different expression. In Greek it is *panteles*, which is there a time term, because there will come a time, when we are in heaven, when we shall no longer require His ability to save. However, regarding 'the uttermost' of our wilderness journey we can always be assured of His ability to save. There will be an end to His need to save but there will never be an end to His love.

In John chapters 1 to 7, the subject matter is **life**. In chapters 8 to 12, it is **light**, Christ illuminating the world. In chapters 13 to 17, it is **love**. Love is mentioned earlier in the Gospel, but in John chapters 13 to 17 there is the circle of divine love. There is the Father's love for the Son, 'thou lovedst me before the foundation of the world', 17. 24. There is the Son's love for the Father, 'that the world may know that I love the Father', 14. 31. There is the Father's love for His own, 'the Father himself loveth you', 16. 27. There is the Son's love for His own in chapter 13 verse 1. There is our love for each other in chapter 13 verse 35. This is the circle of divine love into which His own have been brought by grace, where the Father loves the Son, the Son loves the Father, the Father loves the children, the Son loves His own and we love each other.

'And supper being ended, the devil having now put into the heart of Judas Iscariot, Simon's son, to betray him', v. 2

The thought in 'supper being ended' is 'supper being laid' or 'being come'. Feet are washed before the meal rather than afterwards.

'The devil having now put into the heart of Judas Iscariot, Simon's son, to betray him'. It is the thought that is first put into his heart and then, later, Satan enters into him so that the thought might be carried out, v. 27. There is, therefore, a progression which reaches its climax with Satan entering into him.

It is interesting to observe in connection with Judas that the scripture speaks in John chapter 13 of his heart, v. 2, and of his heel, v. 18, while Luke chapter 22 verse 21 speaks of his hand. Here is the one who has been fully given over to the devil, heart, hand and heel. His full name is

16

also used, 'Judas Iscariot, Simon's son'. His name means 'praise', but he certainly did not live up to its meaning.

It is also very interesting to observe that earlier in the Gospel it is related that Judas was a thief and had the bag, 12. 6. It is tragic to think that a man was prepared as a thief to sell the Son of God for thirty pieces of silver. Exodus chapter 21 verse 32 states that it was the price of compensation that was paid to a man for a slave that had been gored by a bull. This is a great warning against setting one's heart and mind upon money and silver, 'which while some coveted after, they have . . . pierced themselves through with many sorrows', 1 Tim. 6. 10. No doubt there was lingering in Judas's mind the thought that even though he would sell Jesus He would be able to deliver Himself as He had formerly done but when he saw that that was not going to happen there would be remorse.

The word used in the expression 'to betray him' means 'to deliver him up'. In a sense, Judas did not betray Him, and the word does not have that significance, even in 1 Corinthians chapter 11 verse 23. If a person is betrayed, he is unaware of it, but Jesus was not unaware.

John chapter 13 verse 28 makes it clear that the disciples did not perceive what was true of Judas, even when he went out. And when the Lord indicated 'that one of you shall betray me', they 'looked one on another, doubting of whom he spake', vv. 21, 22. They could not think, even then, that it was Judas; and when he went out to sell the Lord Jesus they thought he had gone out to make purchases. In Judas is seen the craft of Satanic camouflage and, undoubtedly, Satan knew his man all along.

'Jesus knowing that the Father had given all things into his hands, and that he was come from God, and went to God', v. 3

The Father had given all things into His hands, yet, in the fullness of that knowledge, He takes the feet of His disciples into these same hands. Every one of these disciples had failed Him and would do so again. Even though He knew these things He took into His hands the feet of Peter, who was going out to deny Him, and Judas, who was going out to sell Him.

It is against the background of knowing that the Father had given all things into His hands, in the full consciousness of His own dignity and majesty, and the greatness of His person, that He goes about His business of washing their feet. In John chapter 10 verses 28 and 29, our Lord said, 'I give unto . . . [my sheep] eternal life; and they shall never perish, neither shall any man pluck them out of my hand. My Father, which gave them me, is greater than all; and no man is able to pluck them out of my Father's hand'. The Revised Version footnote there is very interesting, suggesting, 'That which my Father hath given unto me is greater than all'. This could, perhaps, be seen here. To Him, His own whom the Father had given Him were greater than all else the Father had given Him. In the full knowledge that the Father had given all things into His hands, and that He came from God and was going to God, He rises from supper to wash His disciples' feet.

In John chapter 3 verse 35, the Saviour said, 'The Father loveth the Son, and hath given all things into his hand'. All things were given into His hands in divine purpose away back in eternity but the realization of this will not be until the world to come. There are two thoughts. John speaks of all things being given into His hands; Paul, in Ephesians chapter 1 verse 22, and the writer to the Hebrews, in chapter 2 verse 8, speak of all things under His feet. Both things are true; all things are given into His hands and all things are going to be put under His feet. This will be observed manifestly in the world to come, in His millennial reign, as all things under the feet of the Son of Man speaks of His absolute dominion. However, all things being given into His hands is connected with Him rather as the Son of the Father and has the thought of His disposing of them as He Himself pleases. There is, therefore, not just the idea of dominion, with all things put under His feet, but also that of the disposal of all things as He Himself pleases, as the Son of the Father. Many a son becomes an unworthy heir because he is an unworthy son but the one into whose hands God has placed all things is a worthy heir because He is a worthy Son.

Calvary was not one of the 'all things' given to Him in this verse. It is true that Calvary was a work given to Him by the Father,[1] but the 'all things' here is regarding the Father's gift to Him in terms of the majesty of His person as the heir of all things rather than in terms of a work to do.

In verse 1, it says that He knew that He should depart out of this world unto 'the Father', but in this verse He knew that He 'went to God'. It is when there is introduced the thought of His going to God that we have the action parable in washing their feet. To have communion with Him, as being with God, their feet would need to be washed; there needed to be cleansing.

'He riseth from supper, and laid aside his garments; and took a towel, and girded himself', v. 4

There are seven actions here by the Lord, which have been often interpreted as picturing a down-stooping from heaven to earth, just as seven downward steps are mentioned in Philippians chapter 2.

The garments He laid aside were His upper garments, which would hinder movement in this action of feet washing.

'After that he poureth water into a bason, and began to wash the disciples' feet, and to wipe them with the towel wherewith he was girded', v. 5

The lesson of the towel is that the Lord Jesus completes every work He commences. This is a point that is emphasized particularly in Luke's Gospel. In Luke chapter 7 verse 15, He raises to life the son of the widow of Nain – and then delivered him to his mother. In chapter 9 verse 42, He dispossesses a man of a demon – and then delivered him to his father. In chapter 8 verse 55, He raises the daughter of Jairus – and then said to 'give her meat'. In chapter 15 verse 4, He goes after the

---

[1] See: 'the works which the Father hath given me', John 5. 36; 'I have finished the work which thou gavest me to do', 17. 4.

sheep – until He found it. He completes every work and, thus, will use the towel as well as the basin here.

In the later verses, where He indicates that He has left us this example, it is to be remembered that there is not just the basin to be used by us in washing others' feet but also the towel. The basin was used to wash; the towel was used to wipe. When one washes the feet of another one must also wipe them, in the sense that that is the end of the matter that occasioned the washing of the feet; it is not something to discuss or broadcast.

The Apostle Peter's protest, vv. 6-11

Here the Lord is seen not so much as the Son but as the Prophet and what is emphasized in connection with His being the Prophet is that He is patient. As the patient one He deals with Peter's objection and says, 'What I do thou knowest not now', v. 7; and He also prophesies when He says, 'thou shalt know hereafter', v. 7. The Lord tells Peter that though he did not then understand His actions he would know 'hereafter', or 'after these things', and, in saying this, prophesies that they belong particularly to the day of the Holy Spirit.

'Then cometh he to Simon Peter: and Peter saith unto him, Lord, dost thou wash my feet? Jesus answered and said unto him, What I do thou knowest not now; but thou shalt know hereafter', vv. 6, 7

'Knowest', *eido*, refers to conscious knowledge, a word used frequently by John in his first Epistle. 'Know', *ginosko*, is knowledge gained by experience, that which they would learn. Peter did not understand then, but he would acquire knowledge 'hereafter'. The verse could therefore be rendered, 'What I do thou hast no conscious knowledge of now; but thou shalt learn hereafter'. There are those who have perpetuated literal feet washing but it is made clear here that it was a symbolic act, the significance of which they would know 'after these things'.

'Hereafter' relates to the day of the Spirit, when they would have His enlightenment, by His presence with them, to learn the significance of the feet washing. These words are often taken up and applied to the fact that though the significance of what the Lord is doing is not fully known at present it shall be known when we are with Him. Strictly speaking, however, it is 'what I do thou knowest not' in the matter of feet washing.

Very often feet washing is brought before us as being associated with the present ministry of Christ, perhaps as our Advocate or otherwise, but that is not, in fact, the primary teaching. He said, I have left you an example, that 'ye also ought to wash one another's feet . . . that ye should do as I have done to you', vv. 14, 15. In this action parable He is telling them what they ought to do for each other. Of course, it is true that if we fail each other in the matter of feet washing, He will never fail us; but the main thought here is ministry amongst the saints toward each other.

The water undoubtedly speaks of the word. This ministry is to do with the use of the word, that by which we know the Father and by which we learn of the things that are in our lives that are unsuitable to Him and His presence. It is the use of the word in cleansing each other, not from positive sin but rather from the defilement of the world. As saints meet each other and converse about divine things, they can oftentimes unwittingly cleanse each other from defilement in this world.

'Peter saith unto him, Thou shalt never wash my feet. Jesus answered him, If I wash thee not, thou hast no part with me', v. 8

In 'Thou shalt never wash my feet' the emphasis is on 'Thou' and 'my'. 'Never' is the strongest negative in the Greek language, meaning 'unto the age', eternally, or 'as long as this world lasts'. The reason why Peter said this is that He thought that the Son of God was just giving a lesson in humility. Peter says, in effect, 'Thou, the Son of God from heaven, will never humble Thyself, Lord, to wash my feet, who am but a Galilean fisherman'. The Lord had to point out that it was not just a lesson in humility, telling Peter that if he was not washed he could have no part with Him. It was certainly humility on the part of the Lord to wash their

21

feet, but the lesson was much deeper; that they might have part with Him. There is no doubt that the Lord's actions here would have been a rebuke to their strife as to who should be great, but feet washing is a lesson in cleansing being necessary to communion.

Peter's 'never' is not the same as the Lord's 'never'. Peter's 'never' is sometimes just like ours. We may say that we have learned a lesson and that we will never do that thing again, yet, at times, that is just the very thing that we do. How different is the Lord's 'never'!

'Simon Peter saith unto him, Lord, not my feet only, but also my hands and my head', v. 9

Simon says this after Jesus had explained that there was a significance beyond mere feet washing. He could not bear the thought of being separated from Him, for nothing meant more to him than to have communion with Christ, so he urges Him not just to wash his feet but also his hands and his head.

'Jesus saith to him, He that is washed needeth not save to wash his feet, but is clean every whit: and ye are clean, but not all', v. 10

'He that is washed' refers to the water of new birth, 3. 5, as a result of which we are clean every whit, or everywhere. That is something which cannot be repeated; it was complete in itself, and, thereafter, all that is required is cleansing from defilement by the washing of one's feet. In the consecration of the priesthood Moses acted for God by washing the priests all over. That all-over washing was never repeated. Thereafter, the priests had to have recourse to the laver to cleanse from defilement. The all-over bathing has to do with life, whereas the washing of the feet has to do with communion. The impartation of life by being bathed all over, the new birth, is never repeated; cleansing from defilement, however, must be repeated. The all-over washing is connected to Hebrews chapter 10 verse 22, 'having . . . our bodies washed with pure water', to Titus chapter 3 verse 5, 'the washing of regeneration', and to 1 Corinthians chapter 6 verse 11, 'ye are washed . . . ye are sanctified . . . ye are justified'.

22

There is no thought in the word of God of a fall-away doctrine. Once a person is born again, he is clean every whit in God's sight, although when defilement occurs there is a need for cleansing of the feet.

Judas's feet had been washed, but the Lord Jesus says, 'Ye are not all clean', for Judas had not been bathed.

'For he knew who should betray him; therefore said he, Ye are not all clean', v. 11

The Lord takes up a man on his profession until it becomes apparent that this profession is not real and this is how the fact that the Lord washes Judas' feet is to be understood. It is not until the whole matter is exposed that He says, 'That thou doest, do quickly', v. 27. He washed all their feet, whether they were defiled or not, because He was setting an example. There could still be Judases in the company, but that does not mean to say that we have to treat them as such but to treat them as genuine until their true condition is exposed.

The action parable explained, vv. 12-17

Here the Lord Jesus Christ is not so much seen as Son or Prophet but as Lord because, in verse 14, He speaks of Himself as 'your Lord and Master'. In this connection there is His example and His expectation as far as the disciples are concerned. His example: 'I have given you an example', v. 15; His expectation: 'that ye should do as I have done to you', v. 15.

'So after he had washed their feet, and had taken his garments, and was set down again, he said unto them, Know ye what I have done to you?' v. 12

The meaning of the word 'know', *ginosko*, is 'recognize' or 'perceive' and He asked them therefore whether they perceived what He had done to them.

'Ye call me Master and Lord: and ye say well; for so I am. If I then, your Lord and Master, have washed your feet; ye also ought to wash one another's feet', vv. 13, 14

The Lord altered the order of 'Master', or 'Teacher', and 'Lord'. He is our Lord; we are His servants. It is the matter of obedience. He is our Teacher; we are His disciples. It is the matter of instruction. Matthew chapter 10 verse 24 makes that conclusive, 'The disciple is not above his master [teacher], nor the servant above his lord'. They say, 'Thou art our Teacher and our Lord', but He says, 'I am your Lord and Teacher'. The Lord, of course, gives the correct order. If we are to be benefited and blessed by His teaching, we must first of all be subject to His lordship. This principle is seen in John chapter 7 verse 17, where He said, 'If any man will do his will [He is Lord], he shall know of the doctrine [He is teacher]'. Similarly, in Matthew chapter 11 verse 29, 'Take my yoke upon you [He is Lord], and learn of me [He is teacher]'. Remember that Peter, in verse 8, had said, 'Thou shalt never wash my feet' and he had to learn that a servant never says 'never' to his Lord.

The saints of God in their pathway each day in this world hear things they would better have never heard and see things they would better have not seen. As a result, and despite themselves, they are defiled. It is almost impossible to go a day's journey without being defiled in one way or another. A Christian feels this but then might meet a brother or a sister who will begin to speak about divine things. As far as they are concerned, they cleanse that believer, albeit unwittingly, from the defilement of the world. This connects to the truth of the red heifer in Numbers chapter 19. The same thought is found in, 'the bowels of the saints are refreshed by thee, brother', Philem. 7.

In the example that the Lord gives the disciples He takes their feet into His hands, washes them and wipes them. The force of the example is that, if we are to wash the saints' feet, we have to get down low. When they saw the Son of God down at their feet, and taking their feet into His hands, the first thing that they would think would be that they must mean something to Him. We can never help the saints if they are not aware of the fact that we love them and that they mean something to us.

Using the water is not cleansing in the sense of censure but it is using the word by speaking it. This is a deliberate act if it is following our Lord's example. It is not pointing out where a brother or sister has sinned or failed, for even a carnal brother or sister can use the whip, but rather the imparting of the word of Christ. This makes a person realize just how much there might be in and about him that is unworthy of Christ.

'For I have given you an example, that ye should do as I have done to you', v. 15

In verse 14, it says, 'ye ought' whereas here it says, 'ye should'. The word 'ought' means that 'they owed it as a debt', because of His lordship. Here, however, they should do it because of His example.

'Verily, verily, I say unto you, The servant is not greater than his lord; neither he that is sent greater than he that sent him', v. 16

This is an unalterable principle but, in this verse, it specifically relates to the matter of washing one another's feet. To decline in the matter of feet washing is to set oneself above the Lord. 'The servant is not greater than his lord' appears also in Matthew chapter 10 verse 24 and in John chapter 15 verse 20, in different settings.

'If ye know these things, happy are ye if ye do them', v. 17

The Lord was living this out. To follow His great example brings happiness to His own.

The traitor announced, vv. 18-20

In these verses there is not so much a particular emphasis on the Sonship of the Lord Jesus, as in the first section, but on His deity. He tells His disciples two reasons why He is indicating to them at this time that there was a traitor in their midst. First, He makes a proclamation and a prediction. The proclamation is made that 'ye may believe that I am', v. 19, that they might believe that He is the great 'I am' of eternity. The prediction is noted in the words, 'I tell you before it come to pass',

v. 19 RV. Then, second, in verse 20, the breakdown of Judas, his collapse and treachery, would in no wise invalidate the commission that the Lord had already given to these disciples.

'I speak not of you all: I know whom I have chosen: but that the scripture may be fulfilled, He that eateth bread with me hath lifted up his heel against me', v. 18

It is not the electing grace of God to salvation that is in view here but rather that they were chosen to apostleship. This was 'that the scripture may be fulfilled, He that eateth bread with me hath lifted up his heel against me'. The scripture referred to is Psalm 41 verse 9, where David is speaking of Ahithophel, though the Lord Jesus does not fully quote what David said concerning him. Ahithophel had been David's one-time counsellor but he had turned against him. This aptly describes what was true of Judas. In fact, the whole setting seems to be that of David in these chapters: for example, in chapter 18 Jesus passes over the brook Cedron as David also did in his rejection, but there are also many other parallels.

Judas is referred to twice in the Old Testament, in Psalm 41 verse 9 and Psalm 109 verse 8. Psalm 109 says, 'Let his days be few; and let another take his office', or 'his bishoprick'. That verse is quoted in Acts chapter 1 verse 20. Judas is, of course, referred to in the Gospels, but also in 1 Corinthians chapter 11 verse 23, though not by name. Thus, Judas is brought before us in a threefold way: prophetically in the Old Testament, historically in the Gospels, and doctrinally in 1 Corinthians.

The Lord's reference to the scripture would strengthen the faith of His disciples, as what was going to happen to Him had been predicted. This would also strengthen their confidence in the fact that He was the Messiah. There is the authority of the scriptures in verse 18 but the authority of the 'I am' in verse 19.

'He that eateth bread with me' is literally 'he that eateth my bread', indicating that he was His friend. The sop, in verse 26, would possibly be one of the Passover loaves but here it is 'my bread', bread given to a friend.

26

The lifting up of the heel has the thought of raising the foot, preparing to kick. That was exactly Judas' position here. He had lifted the heel, but the blow had yet to be struck. This would happen when he betrayed the Son of God with a kiss of affection. It is indicative of something that was utterly contemptuous on the part of Judas.

It is remarkable to observe that in this chapter mention is made of Judas' heart, v. 2, and his heel. In Luke chapter 22 verse 21, reference is made to Judas' hand, 'the hand of him that betrayeth me is with me on the table'. Thus, by reference to his hand, heart, and heel, mention is made of the whole man.

'Now I tell you before it come, that, when it is come to pass, ye may believe that I am he', v. 19

The word 'now' is 'from henceforth' or 'from this present time'. He was going to be betrayed with a kiss and so He tells them before it happens so that they might know that He was not just a man. What would happen to Him in relation to His humanity would be a reflection of His deity. By it they would know that He is the great 'I am' of eternity. He was no manipulator of scripture; He told them before it came to pass.

'I am' occurs frequently in John's Gospel. In chapter 8, for example, it occurs in verses 24, 28, and 58. The Lord Jesus Christ is the great 'I am'. 'I am' is God in relation to eternity. When Gods speak of Himself in relation to time and space He says, as in Revelation chapter 1 verse 4, 'him which is, and which was, and which is to come'. In relation to time, He speaks in terms of past, present, and future. In relation to the past, He was. In relation to the present, He is. In relation to the future, He is to come. However, when God speaks of Himself in relation to eternity, He is God who knows no past and no future but one eternal now. God is absolute, immutable, self-existing. Here, the man who was going to be treated in this contemptuous way by Judas was the 'I am' of eternity.

When, in chapter 18, those who came to arrest Him said they were seeking 'Jesus the Nazarene', an expression which would indicate contempt on their part, He said 'I am'. They immediately went backward and fell to the ground, in the august presence of the 'I am' of eternity. The Lord Jesus had said, 'Before Abraham was, I am', 8. 58. An angel could have said, 'Before Abraham was, I was', but the Saviour said, 'Before Abraham was, I am'. That is God apart from time and space. When confronted with cultists who deny the deity of Christ, we do well to remember that the Lord said, 'If ye believe not that I am . . . ye shall die in your sins', 8. 24. All who refuse to accept His deity, that He is the I am of eternity, must die in their sins.

'Verily, verily, I say unto you, He that receiveth whomsoever I send receiveth me; and he that receiveth me receiveth him that sent me', v. 20

Receiving one of His sent ones was to receive the Son, and he who receives the Son receives the Father who sent Him.

In the next chapter He spoke the Father's words and did the Father's works, 14. 10. After He has gone His people do the greater works and also speak His words, v. 12. In the words, 'He that receiveth whomsoever I send', the Lord Jesus is not necessarily thinking of a future sending but of the fact they had already been sent. He is more or less reaffirming and adding to the commission that they have already received. That would indicate that the Lord is assuring them that even though Judas, one of the number, would do such a dreadful thing, their commission would remain unchanged. Everything was not about to collapse and break down. This is a very important word for us today. Sometimes in assembly life a brother or a sister has a breakdown; there is a collapse in their Christian life and testimony. This can make others think that they will have to shut the door, which is not the case. The Lord's words and the Lord's promises remain true to those who will continue faithful to Him.

The self-excommunication of Judas the traitor, vv. 21-30

As to the time, 'it was night', v. 30. John includes throughout his Gospel little expressions like this. He says, 'it was winter', 10. 22; 'it was early', 18. 28; 'it was cold', 18. 18; and, here in chapter 13, He says, 'it was night'.

It is a tense atmosphere in the upper room and an occasion for action rather than words. It almost seems as if the disciples are too afraid to speak. In verse 22, 'the disciples looked one on another, doubting of whom he spake', and they do this without uttering a word. Then, in verse 24, Peter beckons to John, that John should ask Him of whom He spake. Next, in verse 26, Jesus indicated who the traitor was with an action; He gave to the traitor a sop. Finally, in verse 30, Judas goes out from the upper room without uttering a word.

In this section, the Lord and John are heard to speak, but words are few. The Lord speaks in a few words to all the disciples in verse 21, to John in verse 26 and to Judas in verse 27. John speaks in verse 25, but his words are also few.

The various actors are Jesus, His own, John, Peter, Judas, and Satan. John speaks of Jesus in relation to Himself, indicating that 'he was troubled in spirit', v. 21. Then he speaks of Him in relation to His own as He looked upon them and said, 'one of you shall betray me', v. 21. Verse 22 also relates that they 'looked one on another, doubting of whom he spake'. It is amazing to think that these apostles were 'looking one upon another', not questioning what the Lord said but doubting of whom He was speaking. They were not thinking for one moment that it was Judas. John also speaks of his own two-fold posture, leaning on Jesus' bosom, verse 23, and lying on Jesus' breast, verse 25. The correct rendering of both expressions is, in verse 23, 'leaning in Jesus' bosom', and in verse 25, 'lying on Jesus' breast'. John also speaks of Peter, indicating in verse 24 that Peter beckoned to John, that John should ask Him of whom He spake. In verse 27, John speaks of Jesus in relation to Judas, as He says in few words, 'That thou doest, do quickly'. Some render it, 'That thou doest, do more quickly'. Judas went out immediately and it was night. Finally, John also speaks of Satan. After the temptations of our Lord in the wilderness, he departed for a season, but now he returns. In verse 2, the devil put a suggestion into the heart of Judas that he must get on with the plan that was already in his heart; in verse 27, Satan enters into him and takes full possession of the man.

29

'When Jesus had thus said, he was troubled in spirit, and testified, and said, Verily, verily, I say unto you, that one of you shall betray me', v. 21

In chapters 11, 12 and 13, trouble is connected with the Saviour. On the occasion of the death of Lazarus, when Jesus saw Mary weeping and the Jews weeping with her, He groaned in spirit and was troubled, 11. 33. The word 'trouble' there is a little different from what we have here in that it is trouble that expresses itself in a physical way in the body, involving trembling. In chapter 12 verse 27, as He speaks of His death, He says, 'Now is my soul troubled'; He had trouble in relation to His soul. But here, in chapter 13, Jesus 'was troubled in spirit'. He was experiencing trouble in His whole being, in body, soul and spirit.

Here, then, it is important to observe that it is trouble in the spirit and the reason for this was something more than the terrible act of Judas. It was to do with His holiness, that would shrink from such a terrible thing as Judas was going to do, and His love that would cause Him to think, no doubt, of the terrible end that awaited him. It is not for any personal reasons, therefore, that here He is troubled.

However, being who He was He would no doubt think that this was just the beginning of the fulfilment of scripture, and thus His spirit was troubled. There were many scriptures that had yet to be fulfilled, as is noted in chapter 19 verse 28. In the immediate sense it was the betrayal that 'now' troubled His spirit; 'now' means 'from this point of time', suggesting that, while He knew Psalm 41 verse 9 was about to be fulfilled, other scriptures and their fulfilment were also in His mind.

Hatred from the world is to be expected but now He looks away from the world and looks upon one of His own and says, 'one of you'. The amazing thing is that though Jesus was troubled in spirit Judas was not troubled, though he would be later on.

'Then the disciples looked one on another, doubting of whom he spake', v. 22

The word 'doubting' savours the idea of bewilderment. The disciples were completely bewildered that any one of the twelve would ever do such a thing. Remarkably, 'Then the disciples' indicates that even Judas joined in as they looked one on another in bewilderment; and there was nothing about his activity that would indicate his guilt, as verse 29 also shows. He was acting the part and he was therefore acting in the character of those referred to in 2 Corinthians chapter 11 verse 14 as ministers of light. Satan is himself an angel of light.

It says, doubting 'of whom' He spake, not doubting 'what' He spake. They did not question His word, for what He said was truth. Matthew chapter 26 verse 22 says at this juncture that 'they were exceeding sorrowful' and Mark chapter 14 verse 19 that they 'began to be sorrowful'. Matthew chapter 26 verse 22 tells us that now they said, 'Lord, is it I?', but Judas says in verse 25, 'Master [or Rabbi], is it I?' Whereas the others said 'Lord', Judas said, 'Rabbi'.

'Now there was leaning on Jesus' bosom one of his disciples, whom Jesus loved', v. 23

The word 'bosom' means 'a hollow place' whereas, in verse 25, 'breast' is 'the firm part'. The difference is that leaning in the bosom describes John's posture at the time, but he changes his position in verse 25 because of the impact of what the Lord was saying. There, he is not leaning but lying; not in, but on, the breast. Both things are connected with divine love. Leaning in the bosom speaks of the sweetness of divine love; lying on the breast speaks of the security of divine love. There is sweetness always to be enjoyed and there is a sense of security in times of bewilderment and sorrow. We may enjoy this still. It is the secret of divine communication. That is why Peter beckoned to John, as he was leaning in the bosom.

John gives no account of the institution of the Lord's Supper but there is here the spiritual tone and atmosphere of the upper room, without which the Lord's Supper can be cold, formal and meaningless. John's

31

physical posture is indicative of what ought to be the attitude of our spirits. The fact that he is leaning, or reclining, in the bosom indicates that he is set free from the impatience of the flesh, gazing into His face in the enjoyment of communion. This could be our happier, spiritual experience, particularly on a Lord's Day morning.

'Here to rest, so sweetly able,
Occupied alone with Thee'.

In speaking of himself as 'the disciple whom Jesus loved' John does not for one moment mean that Jesus loved him more than the other disciples, for He loved them to the uttermost, v. 1, or that he loved Jesus more than they did. It simply means that John appreciated the tremendous fact that he was loved, *agapao*, by Jesus. John describes himself in this way five times, though in chapter 20 verse 2 a different word, *phileo*, is used for 'loved'.

It is very interesting to observe that though John speaks of himself as 'the disciple whom Jesus loved' on five occasions, three of these, in chapters 13, 19, and 21, are undoubtedly connected. In chapter 13 verse 23, the disciple whom Jesus loved is leaning in the bosom; in chapter 19 verse 26, Jesus saw the disciple whom Jesus loved standing by the cross; in chapter 21 verse 20, the disciple whom Jesus loved is following.

In chapter 13, he is **leaning** in the full consciousness of the fact that he is loved of Jesus, gazing adoringly into His face. In chapter 19, he is **standing** at the cross. The atmosphere of the upper room is filled with divine love but, at the cross, it is charged with the hatred of this world. He could not lean there; this is where he must take his stand, fully conscious of the fact that he is loved of Jesus. For those standing at the cross in chapter 19, it meant that they had completely disassociated themselves from this world's verdict on the Son of God. The world gave Him a cross, but four women and John courageously stand loyal to the one who is on the cross. To take one's stand by the cross today is not any less real for us than it was for John. To disassociate ourselves from the world's verdict on God's Son, and to take a stand by the rejected man, is to separate oneself from the world. There is a need for this.

Fully conscious of the fact of being loved of Him, how could one not take a stand by Him against the world and its verdict? The cross that stands between a person and hell stands between us and the world. Before this cross we stand as lonely strangers; and what makes us accept this 'strangership' is that we are loved of Him.

In chapter 21, the disciple whom Jesus loved is **following** the risen Lord. In verse 19, the Lord said to Peter, 'Follow me'. The Lord did not say to John, 'Follow me', for he was already following in the consciousness of the fact that he was loved of Jesus. It has been said that in John chapter 21 Peter was a conscript but John was a volunteer. He was voluntarily following, conscious of the fact that he was loved of Jesus.

'Simon Peter therefore beckoned to him, that he should ask who it should be of whom he spake', v. 24

Simon Peter beckons to John to take advantage of his near position to ask Him who it was of whom He spake. There is a lot of necessary, practical teaching in this. The secret of divine communication is to lean in His bosom, enjoying nearness to Him. The Lord never shouts His mind to those who are living at a distance but whispers it to those who lean in His bosom in devotion to Him.

There is no shortcut to receiving divine revelation. One might attend all the schools and read all the books but if one is not living near to Him there will be no divine revelation.

'He then lying on Jesus' breast saith unto him, Lord, who is it?' v. 25

In Matthew chapter 26, the others said, 'Lord, is it I?' v. 22, but Judas said, 'Master [or Rabbi], is it I?' v. 25.

Some render this, 'He then having fallen back on the breast of Jesus'. 'Lying' is the same root word as in verse 12, where it is translated 'set down'. John is leaning down on Jesus' breast. Verse 23 describes his permanent posture in the upper room as reclining; in verse 25, because of the bewilderment, he changes his posture so that he is now leaning or lying.

This is necessary for us, too. In ministry on John chapter 20, with reference to the first day of the week when the disciples were gathered together, the doors being shut, we often hear that when we come together, collectively, we must shut the doors to everything that is outside. This is correct and very necessary, but there is another side to it. In Matthew chapter 6 verse 6, the Lord says, 'enter into thy closet, and when thou hast shut thy door'. Being behind the shut door of our own closet in the secret of His presence is as necessary as shutting the door when we gather together.

'Jesus answered, He it is, to whom I shall give a sop, when I have dipped it. And when he had dipped the sop, he gave it to Judas Iscariot, the son of Simon', v. 26

In verses 26 and 27 the traitor is announced. First, his presence is announced and then his person is indicated. Two matters are brought to our attention. On the one hand there is the sop, v. 26, and then there is Satan, v. 27.

The sop would have been from the Passover table. The word 'sop' is derived from the Greek word *psōmion* which means 'to rub' or 'to break' and is used for bread. It would seem that Jesus took a piece of the unleavened bread and dipped it in the gravy connected with the Passover lamb, before giving it to Judas. This was given as a mark of affection to Judas. First of all, then, the Lord appealed to Judas' conscience when He said, 'one of you shall betray me'. However, that made no impact on Judas, who shared with the others in looking one on another doubting of whom He spake. Now it is not an appeal to his conscience but to his affection, in that He gave him what was normally given by the host to a friend, but afterwards Satan entered into him. This appeal to his heart made no impact on Judas as His conscience was seared and his heart hardened, and he went out into the night.

At the end of the chapter, attention is directed to Peter, who would deny the Lord. Peter was a backslider; his conscience was not seared nor his heart hardened. One of the great differences between an apostate and a backslider is that an apostate is quite unimpressed by any divine, spiritual or heavenly influence. This was not the case with Peter. Later, the Lord looked on Peter, who went out and wept bitterly, Matt. 26. 75. Though the Lord gave a sop to Judas, it made no impression, but all that was required for Simon Peter was the look of Jesus. With a backslider there is weakness, but with an apostate there is wilfulness.

'And after the sop Satan entered into him. Then said Jesus unto him, That thou doest, do quickly', v. 27

In verse 2, Satan put the thought into his heart, but now he enters into the man. It was not just that Judas had a demon but rather that he was a demon; he was taken possession of by Satan himself. The word 'then' is 'therefore'. Once Satan had entered into Judas, repentance was no longer possible and, because of this, Jesus says, 'That thou doest, do quickly'.

It is sometimes asked what would have happened if Judas had recanted. It has already been noted that the Lord always deals with a man on the ground of his profession until it becomes apparent that that profession is not real. Here, the Lord goes to the last moment until Satan takes possession of him. The teaching with regard to an apostate in the book of Hebrews will never be understood unless this is accepted. It is only when the person is thoroughly exposed that they are treated on the ground of what they really are. 'Jesus knew from the beginning . . . who should betray him', 6. 64, but patiently bears with him right to the end, until Satan takes possession of the man. We would not have acted towards our betrayer as Jesus did, giving him a sop, but our Lord displays wondrous patience and grace right to the last as He deals with this man.

Judas was not present on the occasion of the institution of the Lord's Supper. Based on Luke's record of the institution of the supper, it is contended that he was, in fact, present. However, it should be observed that Luke gives the institution of the supper in its moral order, and it is introduced as a kind of interpolation, viewed as completely distinct from the Passover, giving its true setting. In Luke's Gospel there are the references to the Passover, then the institution of the supper and then a return to the Passover. That is what makes it appear to some able commentators that Judas was present on that occasion, but actually he went out before the supper was instituted.

It may be safely said that for the institution of the supper the Lord took one of the Passover loaves and one of the three Passover cups. Taking these, He gave them a significance that they never had before, 'This is my body . . . this is my blood', Matt. 26. 26, 28.

'Now no man at the table knew for what intent he spake this unto him. For some of them thought, because Judas had the bag, that Jesus had said unto him, Buy those things that we have need of against the feast; or, that he should give something to the poor', vv. 28, 29

In verses 28 to 30 there is the traitor's exit. The disciples' amazing incredulity and unbelief is recorded, for they could not think for one moment that Judas was the one who would have betrayed the Lord Jesus. Without uttering a word, Judas makes his exit from the upper room. The disciples were significantly mistaken in thinking that Judas had gone out to buy those things that they had need of against the feast or that he should give something to the poor. The opposite was the case. Judas had not gone out to buy, but to sell; he had not gone out to give, but to receive. He had gone out to sell the Son of God and to receive in exchange thirty pieces of silver. They could never think that Judas would do this; he was so clever in his hypocrisy that they never detected a thing.

To 'buy those things that we have need of against the feast' poses a problem if it is the Passover. The word 'feast' is used on occasions with regard to the Passover and on other occasions it is used with regard to the feast of unleavened bread; sometimes it comprehends both. Here, it is best understood as comprehending both the feasts of Passover and unleavened bread.

It might well be that Judas had in mind that he would betray the Lord and obtain money but that the Lord would have delivered Himself from this situation, as He had in different situations in the past.

In that they thought that Judas had gone out to get something to give to the poor, there is indicated that this was a habit of Jesus and His disciples. Paul says in Acts chapter 20 verse 35 'to remember the words of the Lord Jesus, how he said, It is more blessed to give than to receive'. It is evident that this was a custom of Jesus, one that He taught His disciples. In Galatians chapter 2 verses 9 and 10, they gave to Paul and Barnabas the right hands of fellowship, enjoining them to remember the poor.

The state of Judas' heart was indicated by the fact that he thought Mary was able to break her alabaster box of ointment and wipe the Lord's feet only by not giving to the poor. In fact, the thirty pieces of silver was only ten per cent of the cost of Mary's ointment. Mary lavished this vast sum on His person and Judas was going out to sell Him for only one tenth of the cost of ointment. Judas was prepared to sell the Son of God for the price that was paid in compensation for a slave that had been gored by an ox, Exod. 21. 32.

'He then having received the sop went immediately out: and it was night', v. 30

That 'it was night' symbolizes what, in fact, was his eternal portion. He was like Cain, who 'went out from the presence of the Lord', Gen. 4. 16; Judas becomes a man who has 'gone in the way of Cain', Jude 11.

The Lord announces His departure to His disciples, vv. 31-35

In connection with the announcement of His own departure there are two precious truths. First, as the Son of man He was going to be glorified in heaven, vv. 31, 32. Second, He intended to be glorified on the earth in His disciples, vv. 33-35.

Once Judas has gone out the atmosphere in the upper room clears. Whatever restraint there had been by the presence of Judas had now been removed and Jesus is no longer occupied with his treachery. Instead, He begins to speak to His disciples about His death, resurrection and exaltation. He tells them that His going back to God and being glorified by Him in heaven would involve Him being separated from them. He says, in verse 33, 'Little children, yet a little while I am with you'.

In chapter 12, thinking of Calvary, He was troubled in His soul; in chapter 13, thinking of the betrayal by Judas, He was troubled in His spirit; but now He is thinking of the result of His death and therefore strikes a different note. He speaks in terms of Himself being glorified and God being glorified in Him.

'Therefore, when he was gone out, Jesus said, Now is the Son of man glorified, and God is glorified in him', v. 31

In verses 31 and 32, there are four of the most profound statements in the scriptures concerning our Lord Jesus Christ. These statements are, 'Now is the Son of man glorified', 'God is glorified in him', 'God shall . . . glorify Him in himself' and 'God . . . shall straightway glorify him'.

'Now is the Son of man glorified'. In chapter 11, reference is made to the glorification of the Son of God and, in chapter 17, to the glorification of the Son of the Father, but, in chapter 13, to the glorification of the Son of man.

In chapter 11, the Son of God is glorified by raising a man from the dead, but, in chapter 13, the Son of man is glorified by Himself submitting to death, in which God, too, was glorified. At Calvary there was the greatest display of the intrinsic work of the Son of man against the background of man's hatred and Satan's power. We often think of Calvary merely in terms of what it means to us, but it was, in fact, the glorification of the Son of man in the manifestation of His intrinsic worth and excellency. This was not just by His power over death but by submitting Himself to it.

This is the standpoint from which the death of Christ is viewed in John's Gospel. It does not have the sin offering aspect of the death of Christ, which is the death of Christ for our blessing and our eternal good, in view, but rather, the death of Christ from the standpoint of the burnt offering, that in it the Son of man is glorified and God is glorified.

In John's Gospel, He says, in chapter 10 verse 17, 'Therefore doth my Father love me, because I lay down my life, that I may take it again'. In His death there is seen the Father's love towards Him. Again, in chapter 14 verse 31, He says, 'But that the world may know that I love the Father . . . let us go hence'. In death there was the proof of His love for the Father. We are inclined to forget this aspect of the death of Christ; He goes into death in the enjoyment of His Father's love and to prove conclusively His love to the Father. This burnt offering aspect of the death of Christ is also seen in chapter 12. 'Now is my soul troubled; and what shall I say? Father, save me from this hour: but for this cause came I unto this hour. Father, glorify thy name', 12. 27, 28. He is saying, 'Glorify thy name in my death'. If we read and study the offerings, we will discover that they open up aspects of the death of Christ that are seldom touched upon or understood by many of the Lord's people.

In John's Gospel, there is no record of the garden, His agony, His sweat and His prostration, or of the angel visiting Him to strengthen Him. In fact, in John's Gospel it is not Jesus who is prostrate in the dust of the earth but those who came to arrest Him, who went backward and fell down to the ground in the presence of the great I AM. In John's record of His trial we might almost feel sorry for Pilate, who is quailing not because of his wife's dream, as in other Gospels, but because he discovers himself in the august presence of the I AM. Further, John's record of the crucifixion makes no reference to the hours of darkness, to the last pardon of the dying thief, or to His cry, 'Why hast thou forsaken me'. John was able to record these things because he was one of those last five who stood at the foot of the cross, yet he makes no mention of any of them. John also makes no mention of Simon the Cyrenian being compelled to carry His cross; in chapter 19, He is bearing His own cross. The burnt offering aspect of John is also seen in chapter 20 verse 17, where He says to Mary, 'Touch me not; for I am not yet ascended to my Father'.

39

It is our common lot that we are the sons of men, but He became the Son of man in a unique way. We are the sons of God, but He is the Son of God in a unique way. We are sons of God by regeneration and by adoption, but He is the Son of God essentially and eternally. 'Son of man' is an official title of the Lord Jesus Christ relative to Him carrying out the purpose of God in this earth. As the Son of man, He is presented in connection either with His reproach and suffering or with His exaltation. He is the Son of man lifted up, who suffers; and He is the Son of man who is going to come in glory.

In chapter 12 verse 23, the reference is to the official glory of the Son of man, in connection with the kingdom, bringing forth much fruit: but here it is the glory of the Son of man morally, the intrinsic worth and excellence of the Son of man upon the tree.

'God is glorified in Him' because in His death divine counsels could be realized which had hitherto remained unaccomplished, and in Him, in His death, there is perhaps the greatest manifestation of the attributes of God. Nowhere are divine holiness and divine love seen as at the place called Calvary.

The fact that He speaks of His death is confirmed by verse 32, where it speaks of Him being 'straightway' glorified. His death is viewed, as it is throughout the upper room ministry, as something that is past, an accomplished fact. This is also the case in chapter 17, where He says, 'I have finished the work which thou gavest me to do'; the reference is to the cross, viewed as a finished work.

'If God be glorified in him, God shall also glorify him in himself, and shall straightway glorify him', v. 32

God was glorified in Him on the cross, 'God shall also glorify him in himself' in His exaltation. 'In' Himself, rather than 'with' Himself', is an unusual statement. It refers to a particular glorification, which is God glorifying Him in His own view of glory, glorifying Him in God's own joy, glorifying Him now in God's throne in heaven. 'Shall' does not refer to something that lies still in the future, but it is the 'shall' of argument, in the context of 'if'.

40

'And [God] shall straightway glorify him'. This amplifies the previous statement by adding the thought that this would immediately happen. God could not wait to do this. He is not yet upon the throne of David, nor yet on any other throne, but He is glorified in God's glory.

The Son of man glorifies God on the cross and God, in turn, glorifies the Son. In fact, Calvary made God a debtor to His Son, to glorify Him; and all the glory the Son brought to God from the cross finds its perfect answer in all the glory that He has in heaven now. It was a debt that God gladly and immediately paid. It is perfectly true that there are glories that shall yet be lavished upon Him eternally, but this verse is referring to something that is positional at this present time.

These must necessarily be acquired glories, as the subject matter is the Son of man.

'Little children, yet a little while I am with you. Ye shall seek me: and as I said unto the Jews, Whither I go, ye cannot come; so now I say to you', v. 33

In the first Epistle of John, the expression 'little children' occurs seven times, but only once in the Gospel. It is a diminutive of affection, not of age. A diminutive of age calls a distinction between different persons, some older and some younger, but a diminutive of affection embraces all of God's people. Here, it seems it was addressed particularly to the disciples.

It might well be that the Lord is anticipating what is in His heart in chapter 14 verse 18, when He says to them, 'I will not leave you orphans' JND. His heart is going out to them; He would not leave them as orphans in this world in the little while until He comes again, Heb. 10. 37. He said, 'I will come to you', 14. 18. Had He not come to them they would have been left as orphans in the world. Mary would have been left weeping, Thomas doubting, the disciples fearful, the Emmaus two disillusioned, but they were His dear children and He came to them. Here, however, He says, 'Little children, yet a little while I am with you'.

'Ye shall seek me' does not refer to seeking Him in the sense of seeking Him in prayer but in view of His bodily absence. They did this after His death, at the sepulchre.

The word 'Jews' is used technically, here, of the whole nation as distinct from Gentiles, though sometimes it is used only of the tribes of Judah and Benjamin. He had said to the Jews, 'Whither I go, you cannot come', but He does not say that to the disciples. He is referring to His going to the Father, and, further down, He says, 'ye shall follow me afterwards'.

'A new commandment I give unto you, That ye love one another; as I have loved you, that ye also love one another', v. 34

In this delightful section the Lord Jesus gives the disciples an edict and an example, and tells them of an effect. The edict is, 'A new commandment I give unto you, That ye love one another'. He sets before them an example, 'that ye love one another; as I have loved you'. The effect is that, 'By this shall all men know that ye are my disciples, if ye have love one to another', v. 35.

In John's Gospel, the Jews are seen as His enemy and thus He says to them, 'Whither I go you cannot come'. Now, He gives to His own something distinct, a new commandment, that they love one another as He has loved them.

'A new commandment I give unto you'. It is remarkable that He finds it necessary to command them to love. This is because of the flesh, which is in all of us, and can make us suspicious and envious of each other. Loving one another is not natural, being something that is even beyond mere etiquette; it is divine. It is solemn that He should command them to love one another because failure to love then becomes disobedience to a divine edict, which makes the result murder.

The command to love was not new. The law said, 'Thou shalt love thy neighbour as thyself'. Our Lord's commandment is new, however, because never had the command to love had such a motive, 'as I have loved you'. It is not 'even as' in the sense of 'in exactly the same way', but it gives the reason for it, which is that He loved us. The word 'new'

42

is not new in contrast to old but fresh in contrast to that which is now worn out.

It is true that to love in this sense is the result of the operation of the Holy Spirit in us, but it is the Epistles that indicate this. In the Epistles we learn of the power in which this love is to be expressed. Nothing that we do for God is done apart from the Spirit, though this is not dealt with here. It must be remembered that the particular course to understanding the scriptures is reading in context.

'By this shall all men know that ye are my disciples, if ye have love one to another', v. 35

He is going to be separated from them by being glorified by God in heaven. His great desire is that He should be glorified in them, here on the earth, by all men knowing that they are His disciples by their love one to another.

'My disciples' is not just in terms of possession, the disciples belonging to Him; rather, character is in view. The word is, 'disciples of mine', with the significance, 'by this shall all men know that ye are my disciples indeed'.

What marks us out as being His disciples indeed is not a profession of standing for the truth or wearing a badge but love one to another. People outside might think that the saints are a strange people with a lot about them that is not understood or agreed with, but one thing about them is that they certainly love one another. We must think of how people esteem us and ensure that, as the world looks on, they see that this is true of us. Love one for another is undoubted evidence that we are indeed the Lord's.

Dialogues between Christ and His disciples, v. 36 – 14. 24

The dialogues that Christ has are: with Peter, 13. 36 - 14. 4; Thomas, 14. 5-7; Philip, 14. 8-21; and Judas, not Iscariot, 14. 22-24.

These dialogues arose as a result of the Lord Jesus being interrupted by these disciples as He was speaking. Three of these interruptions were in the nature of questions and one was a request. They must be considered against the disciples' Jewish background and their Jewish expectations.

The questions by Simon Peter and Thomas make it evident that both of these disciples could only think of a **material** place to which God's Son was going. That is why Peter asked the question, '**whither** goest thou?' and Thomas, 'we know not **whither** thou goest and how can we know the way?' In reply, God's Son showed that there was more involved than going to a material place for He was, in fact, going back to a person.

The interruptions by Philip and Judas make it evident that with their particular Jewish background they could only think in terms of the **physical** side. Philip said, '**shew** us the Father and it sufficeth us' and Judas, 'Lord, how wilt thou **manifest** thyself unto us, and not unto the world?' Philip thought that if only they could have a theophany, if only they could but see the Father, it would be a befitting inauguration to His kingdom. Judas had in his mind that the manifestation of God's Son to the world would also be in keeping with the establishment of His kingdom.

'Simon Peter said unto him, Lord, whither goest thou? Jesus answered him, Whither I go, thou canst not follow me now; but thou shalt follow me afterwards', v. 36

The first dialogue is with Simon Peter, from this verse to chapter 14 verse 4. Simon's question stems from the statement in verse 33, 'Whither I go, ye cannot come', where the Lord was repeating what He formerly had said to the Jews in chapter 7 verse 34. The Lord said many other things to the disciples but evidently His intimation of His going away weighed most heavily in the heart of Simon Peter, even more so than the new commandment that the Lord had just given to them, that they should love one another.

The Lord did not answer Simon's question, though this was not because the disciples knew where He was going. The KJV suggests that

44

in chapter 14 verse 4, when the Lord said, 'whither I go ye know, and the way ye know', the disciples knew where He was going. However, the RV rendering is, 'And whither I go, ye know the way', indicating not that they knew where He was going but that they knew the way.

The response to Simon Peter's question discloses to them certain facts connected with His going away. First, there was the matter of them following Him. How precious it was for the disciples to know that though He was going away they would follow Him, if not now then afterwards. Second, He tells them not only that He is going but also the reason for this, which was that He was going to prepare a place for them.

The Lord discloses that there are two matters that will happen afterwards. In verse 7, He said, 'What I do thou knowest not now; but thou shalt know hereafter'. Then, in this verse, 'thou shalt follow me afterwards'. The Lord is making it clear that His destination is the Father and the Father's house, but that He will go there by the way of the cross. The cross was in a unique way the Saviour's cross. Accordingly, neither Simon nor the apostles could follow Him now; as a Saviour He must go to the cross alone, but they would follow Him afterwards. How precious must this indication have been to the disciples that this separation was not going to be permanent. If He says to the unconverted Jews in verse 33, 'Whither I go, ye cannot come', He says to the disciples, '[Ye shall] follow me afterwards'.

It is possible that this is the first indication that Simon Peter would become a martyr, although the statement has a broader significance than this. In chapter 21, Simon Peter stands between youth and old age. The Lord says in verse 18, 'When thou wast young, thou girdedst thyself, and walkedst whither thou wouldest [by his own will]: but when thou shalt be old, thou shalt stretch forth thy hands, and another shall gird thee [in chains], and carry thee [to a martyr's death] whither thou wouldest not'. What characterized him in youth was self-confidence and self-will, but what would characterize him in old age would be his being led whither he 'wouldest not'. In former days, he had protested that he would die for Christ but had failed; in his old age he would be led whither he wouldest not but in the death that he would die he would glorify God. In the strength of restoring grace, he would do what he had said he would do in His own strength, but had failed.

'Peter said unto him, Lord, why cannot I follow thee now? I will lay down my life for thy sake', v. 37

Simon thinks that following Him means death with Him and so he says, 'I will lay down my life for thy sake'. In Mark chapter 14 verse 31, the other disciples protested in a similar way to Simon Peter. After Peter had been told that he would deny the Lord three times, Simon Peter vehemently said to the Lord, 'If I should die with thee, I will not deny thee in any wise'. Mark adds, 'Likewise also said they all'.

Peter said this in reliance upon his own strength. He was a man who went from one extreme to the other. At first, he said to the Lord, 'Thou shalt never wash my feet', but then he said, 'not my feet only, but also my hands and my head', 13. 8, 9. Again, in the garden of Gethsemane, in the presence of armed men, he drew a sword and cut off a man's ear, 18. 10. Later, in the presence of a maid, he denied the Lord. In Peter we see both the strength and the weakness of the flesh and learn that the flesh is of no avail either in its weakness or its strength. What Peter says here was false courage, because he said it in the strength of the flesh, and the flesh, unfortunately, never leaves us.

It is better, however, to be zealous rather than complacent. When, in chapter 21, Simon said to the Lord, 'Lord . . . thou knowest that I love thee', he was saying to the Lord that even when he denied Him he still loved Him. Though others might speak against Peter and condemn him, he was confident that the Lord knew this with His insight, and could read his heart.

It is interesting that the thought of laying down one's life is peculiar to John's writings. The Lord speaks in chapter 10 verse 15 of the good shepherd laying down His life for the sheep and in 1 John chapter 3 verse 16 it says that 'we ought to lay down our lives for the brethren'.

'Jesus answered him, Wilt thou lay down thy life for my sake? Verily, verily, I say unto thee, The cock shall not crow, till thou hast denied me thrice', v. 38

In Luke chapter 22 verse 34, and here, it is said that this prediction was made by the Lord in the upper room. In Matthew chapter 26 verse 34 and Mark chapter 14 verse 30, Matthew and Mark state that this prediction happened between the upper room and Gethsemane. Of course, the answer might be that the Lord found it necessary to say this twice to Simon Peter.

Mark states that the cock would crow twice and that this prediction by Jesus made Simon Peter to be more vehement. It is accepted, and rightly so, that Mark received his details from the Apostle Peter; Peter speaks of Marcus as 'my son', 1 Pet. 5. 13. No doubt Peter told Mark that the Lord told him that the cock would crow twice and that, when the Lord Jesus told him this, he became more vehement. Thus, Simon Peter speaks for himself. Of course, a great deal has been said about the cock crowing twice. Some have suggested that Peter did not hear the first cock-crowing and that he only heard the second. However, Mark chapter 14 verse 30 says, 'This day, even in this night, before the cock crow twice, thou shall deny me thrice'. It was before the cock crowed twice that Simon denied the Lord thrice.

Others have suggested that the cock crowing here refers to one of the watches. Mark chapter 13 verse 35 speaks of the 'cockcrowing' as being the third watch of the night. Here, however, it is the actual crowing of a cock that is referred to and the fact that Mark tells us the cock would crow twice eliminates all thought of this being the third watch of the night. When it is the watch that is referred to it is one word that is used, the 'cockcrowing', but here it is two words, the 'crowing of the cock'. I believe that we have here the Lord Jesus muzzling the cock so that it only crowed by the Lord's command and at the appropriate moment.

The Lord having dominion over creation is an interesting subject. He had dominion here over the fowl of the air; in Matthew chapter 17, John chapter 21 and Luke chapter 5, He had dominion over the fish in the sea; and when He rode into Jerusalem on an untamed colt, the colt the

47

foal of an ass on which never man sat, He exercised dominion over the beast of the field.

Indeed, Peter did deny His Lord thrice. Matthew states, in chapter 26 verse 74, that he began 'to curse and to swear'. His cursing was the pronouncement of anathemas as he denied the Lord; his swearing was the taking of an oath that he knew not the man. This was very sad, but we do well not so much to condemn Peter as to search our own hearts.

Chapter 14

The chapter divides into two sections. In verses 1 to 14, the emphasis is on faith, the word 'believe' occurring in verses 1, 10, 11 and 12. In verses 15 to 31, the emphasis is upon love, as noted in verses 21, 23, 24, 28 and 31.

Another way to view the chapter is that in verses 1 to 3 the emphasis is upon the Son and involves hope; in verses 4 to 14 the emphasis is upon the Father and involves faith; but in verses 15 to 26 the emphasis is upon the Holy Spirit and involves love.

However, there is not only emphasis upon hope, faith and love but also upon the matter of 'abode' and 'abiding'. As far as being in this world was concerned, verse 10, the Father was abiding in the Son and as far as the disciples were concerned the Spirit of truth was abiding along with them. That which would characterize His absence from them is that 'My Father and I will make our abode with you', v. 23. This would be by the Holy Spirit. Then, with regard to the future, there is His coming again, v. 2, 'In my Father's house are many mansions'. He uses the same word as above, many 'abodes'.

'Let not your heart be troubled: ye believe in God, believe also in me', v. 1

The emphasis in these verses is on the Son. Note the repeated references to 'I' and 'myself'. In verse 2, 'I go'; in verse 3, 'I will come again'; in verse 3, 'and receive you unto myself'; again, in verse 3, 'that where I am, there ye may be also'; in verse 6, 'I am the way, the truth, and the life'. Over these verses may be put the heading 'hope'. Our Lord speaks of the blessed hope of His return in verse 3 when He says, 'I will come again, and receive you unto myself'.

The Lord's dialogue with Peter continues from chapter 13. Many things had happened in the upper room that would, no doubt, have troubled the hearts of all His disciples. The heart is the seat of feeling and of faith. He had announced the presence of a traitor, Judas, in their midst and He had had to tell Peter that he would deny Him. However, what

49

troubled them most was His statement that He was going to leave them, 13. 33, and that they could not follow Him now, v. 36. However, He is going to tell them that the day is coming when He would come again.

The statement of the Lord Jesus, 'Let not your heart be troubled', must be considered against the background that, in chapter 11 verse 33, chapter 12 verse 27 and chapter 13 verse 21, He had Himself been troubled in body, soul and spirit. Those who have themselves experienced trouble are best equipped to comfort those who are troubled. Though He was experiencing great trouble at this time, this does not occupy His heart; His selflessness is seen in His great desire that His disciples should not be troubled.

'Ye believe in God, believe also in me' is an amazing statement of the Son of God. Here we have evidence of His deity, for no mere man could ever place himself alongside God as an object of man's trust. The reason why the Saviour said this was that He had told them that He was going away; soon, they would not see Him. He reminds them it would not be a new experience for them to believe in one whom they could not see, for they believed in God, as did the Old Testament saints. Now, they were to continue to believe in Him, though unseen, even as they had always believed in God whom they had never seen. There is no rebuke here; He was simply indicating to them that they would continue to do what they had always been doing, but with a different object of faith.

There is a peculiar blessing for those who believe in a Saviour they have never seen. The Lord Jesus said, 'blessed are they that have not seen, and yet have believed', John 20. 29. Peter takes the matter a little further when he says, 'Whom having not seen, ye love', 1 Pet. 1. 8. To love a person we have never seen is something which naturally speaking we would not care to do. However, having already put our trust in Him, we love Him though we have never seen Him.

In verse 1, He speaks of God, but, in verse 2, He speaks of the Father. In the Old Testament, they believed in God rather than the Father, e.g., Abram believed God, Gen. 15. 6, and God was not ashamed to be called 'their God', Heb. 11. 16. In the Old Testament, they believed in God without believing in the Son, because the Son had not then been revealed as a Saviour, but, in New Testament times, it is impossible to believe in the Son without believing in God.

The questions asked in this chapter seem to indicate that the disciples had not entered into the significance of His going away, of His Father's house and of His manifesting Himself to the world. A Jew had never anticipated believing in an unseen Messiah, for the Jewish expectation was a Messiah here on the earth sitting in His kingdom, ruling from the river to the sea. Now, however, He asked them to believe in an unseen Messiah.

'In my Father's house are many mansions: if it were not so, I would have told you. I go to prepare a place for you', v. 2

He has already spoken about His Father's house in this gospel. He previously said, 'make not my Father's house an house of merchandise', 2. 16, but here it is somewhat different. That typical house at Jerusalem had been desecrated and had been rejected by Him. Now, He speaks of the anti-typical house, the true house in heaven to which He was going, which cannot be desecrated.

It may be the case that Thomas, when he said, 'Lord we know not whither thou goest; and how can we know the way?' had made the mistake of confusing the Father's house to which our Lord refers and the Father's house at Jerusalem. He could not understand heavenly things and was, possibly, connecting His going away with His going to the royal city and the Father's house there. Thomas and Philip are taken up with the earthly and temporal, though it might be that they were thinking of the prophet who said, 'mine house shall be called an house of prayer for all people', Isa. 56. 7. That is yet future and it is possible that they thought of the Father's house from that standpoint.

The word 'heaven' occurs in both the plural and the singular. The three heavens are: the aerial heavens, which are the atmospheric heavens above and around us; the stellar heavens; and the eternal, uncreated heaven. When the word occurs in the plural it can refer to the atmospheric and stellar heavens, or to the three heavens. The uncreated heaven is the abode of God and of the high, holy angelic

51

beings, and is spoken of in Hebrews chapter 9 verse 24 as 'heaven itself'. Heaven itself, the abode of God, has been constituted the Father's house for us by there being there, now, a man in a body. The fact that the Son is there in all the wondrous reality of His manhood has made heaven itself the Father's house, to which we will one day be taken.

There is something sweet about the Lord saying not 'in the Father's house' but 'in my Father's house'. The Lord tells them He has a home, 'my Father's house', and one day He would come for them and take them there. His home is going to be our home. He would never impart to our hearts a hope that could ever be disappointed or that He could never fulfil. In 2 Corinthians chapter 5 verse 8, the Apostle Paul speaks of being absent from the body and at home with the Lord.

'Paradise' is the same place as the Father's house, but with the distinction that it belongs to the disembodied or unclothed state in which the soul is dispossessed of the body. Each of the three occurrences of the word 'paradise' in the New Testament is related to the disembodied state. Paul was caught up into paradise and says, 'whether in the body, or out of the body, I cannot tell', 2 Cor. 12. 3. Jesus said to the dying thief, 'To day shalt thou be with me in paradise', Luke 23. 43. The Lord and the dying thief went to paradise but clearly not in the body. Paradise belongs to the disembodied state.

The place that He prepares for His church is one of the many mansions, or abiding places. These are for families. In Ephesians chapter 3 verse 15, Paul prays to the Father, of whom 'every family in heaven and on earth is named' RV; there are going to be families in heaven and on earth. In His Father's house there are abodes for every family, as there shall be for families on earth. Old Testament saints shall have an abode; martyred saints of the tribulation shall have an abode; I believe children that have died before the age of responsibility, who are not in the church, will have their particular abode; and we too shall have our abode. Isaiah chapter 19 verse 25 speaks of three of the families that shall be on earth in the coming kingdom when it says, 'Blessed be Egypt my people, and Assyria the work of my hands, and Israel mine inheritance'.

There is no thought of one having a bigger abode than another because of greater faithfulness; in the Father's house there is no distinction, as it is all of grace. There is no reward connected to the Father's house; this is, rather, connected with the Judgement Seat of Christ and with His appearing and His kingdom.

The Father's house is not exclusively and entirely a heavenly thought. There will be those who enjoy the Father's house in the heavenly sphere who are not of the church and who will revert to the earth in the eternal state, whilst the church retains its heavenly character and its heavenly position.

The lovely statement, 'if it were not so I would have told you', has a delightful human touch. He is really saying that He would never deceive them. How good it is to know that we have a Saviour who would never deceive us.

'I go to prepare a place for you' does not mean that He is actively engaged in building our abode in the sky. His preparing it just involves His presence there as a man, something which was never so before. There is now in heaven a man, in a body, and so the place is prepared for sinners saved by grace also to be there in bodies. 'Whither the forerunner is for us entered, even Jesus', Heb. 6. 20, speaks of this. This verse is against the background of the Old Testament and the day of atonement, when the high priest entered alone. In Leviticus chapter 16, no man could be there with him and no man was to follow him, but the Saviour has entered as a forerunner, assuring us that we will also be there. In the meantime, He is preparing a people for the place that is already prepared. He is not preparing a people in terms of fitness or in terms of their fidelity; they are prepared the moment they put their trust in Him.

There are those who teach that His going to prepare a place is in reference to His going to Calvary. He went there to prepare the people for the place, but His going to heaven is to prepare the place for the people. The fact that He is not referring to Calvary is clear in that He speaks in verse 3 not only of going to the place but of coming again

53

from it. He did not go to Calvary and then come for them, but He has gone to heaven and He will come for us.

This is very different from Revelation chapter 12 verse 6, where, with regard to the godly remnant of the nation of Israel, we read, 'And the woman fled into the wilderness, where she hath a place prepared of God'. That remnant shall be preserved by God through the days of the great tribulation in the place prepared by God for them, in the wilderness. The place that is prepared for us, however, is the Father's house.

'And if I go and prepare a place for you, I will come again, and receive you unto myself; that where I am, there ye may be also', v. 3

The purpose for which He comes again is brought before us in a unique way in John chapter 14. His coming is viewed as being not just for our blessing but for the satisfaction of His own heart. It will be the Son's great pleasure that His own will be with Him where He is.

There is no expression of doubt in the use of 'if'. The Lord's coming is guaranteed by the fact of His departure; the fact that He was going was a guarantee that He would come again. Both His going and His coming have the disciples in view. He was going to prepare a place for them, and He was coming again to receive them.

In verse 17, the word 'receive' occurs again in the phrase, 'Even the spirit of truth; whom the world cannot receive', but there the Lord employs a slightly different word. In verse 3, the word involves the Lord giving expression to the deep desire of His heart to receive to Himself those for whom He is going to come. He is coming, not just to receive us but to receive us to Himself, to make us near to Himself. It is with this in view that He will come and receive them, that 'where I am, there ye may be also'. This ought to touch our hearts. It will certainly be our crowning joy, but it shall be, at the same time, the great pleasure of the Son to receive us unto Himself.

'I will come again' is, in the King James Version, in the future tense though it is translated elsewhere in the present tense, 'I am coming again' or 'I come again'. For this reason, some have suggested that all that is involved here is a continual coming of God's Son, in this present day, by the Spirit, to Christians. However, that is not the significance of the present tense. There are two thoughts here. First, He says, 'I go' and 'I come', indicating that there is nothing between, in the sense that between His going and His coming there are no prophecies which have to be fulfilled. This era of divine grace belongs not to the prophetic calendar. Second, and this is the main thought, the present tense, 'I go' is employed to indicate the certainty of His coming again.

When we remember the Jewish background of the disciples, we can only feebly understand the tremendous impact that these words of the Saviour must have had upon them. They had only thought of an earthly Messiah setting up His kingdom here on the earth and gathering His own around Him; His coming to receive them to Himself in the place to which He was going was something they had never thought of before this moment.

'And whither I go ye know, and the way ye know', v. 4

The Revised Version rendering of this is, 'And whither I go, ye know the way'. It is evident from subsequent interruptions that they were not quite sure as to where He was going, but they knew the way.

'Thomas saith unto him, Lord, we know not whither thou goest; and how can we know the way?' v. 5

The Lord's dialogue with Thomas is found in verses 5 to 7. Thomas was the one who said, 'Let us also go, that we may die with him', 11. 16. The disciple who was prepared to go with Jesus and to die with Him now asks the question, 'Lord, we know not whither Thou goest; and how can we know the way?' Thomas is telling the Lord that He still has not told them the place to which He is going and asks, therefore, how they can know the way. In His reply the Son of God makes it clear that it is not a place to which He is going; it is, of course, true that He was going to prepare a place for them but He wanted Thomas to understand that it

55

was a person, the Father, to whom He was going. This causes the Son of God to make three profound statements in verse 6, in which He states, 'I am the way' to the Father, 'the truth' about the Father and 'the life' from the Father. In verse 7, He further informs Thomas that the Father is not just 'the' Father but He is 'my' Father, and that if he had known, or recognized, the Son he would have known 'my Father' also. That would have settled the question as to where He was going and to where, one day, they would follow Him.

What seems to have been on Thomas' mind was that the Father's house was in Jerusalem, for it is evident Thomas thought no further than an earthly Messiah with His earthly people. The issue that was on his mind was how he could know the way.

'Jesus saith unto him, I am the way, the truth, and the life: no man cometh unto the Father, but by me', v. 6

He is indicating to Thomas that He is going to a person, the Father, and to this person He, the Son of God, is the way. He is also, in Himself, the revelation of the truth of the Father. He is also the life in which the truth of the Father can be enjoyed. These are profound statements. He is the personification of the way, and of the truth, and of the life.

'I am the way'. 'I' is emphatic. The Lord is not saying, 'I make the way to the Father' or 'I reveal the way to the Father' but 'I am, in Myself, the way to the Father'. Note also, He does not say that He is the way to God but the way to the Father. He is not merely thinking of eventually being the way to the Father; He is the way to the Father, now and always.

As far as we are concerned, the order would be 'life' first, because that is where we begin; then 'truth', the revelation of the Father; and, then, there is the way to the Father. However, the Lord begins with the fact that 'I am the way', because Thomas had asked the question, 'How can we know the way?'

'I am ... the truth'. Chapter 1 tells us that the truth came by Him and in chapter 8 His teaching was truth, but here He is Himself the personification of the truth. The truth of the Father can only be learned in Him.

'I am . . . the life'. He is truly the personification of life. Chapter 1 says, 'In him was life'. In chapter 5 verse 21, He says that He 'quickeneth whom he will'. In chapter 11 verse 25, He says, 'I am the resurrection, and the life'. Those who believe have life in Him.

The Lord is emphasizing that there is something greater than a place, namely the Father; and that coming to the Father is greater than coming to the Father's house.

'If ye had known me, ye should have known my Father also: and from henceforth ye know him, and have seen him', v. 7

There is a gentle rebuke to Philip in this verse.

'If ye had known me' has the significance, 'If ye had recognized me, if you had come to know me through the recurring revelations of myself, you would have a certain knowledge of my Father also'. In the first clause the emphasis is upon the verb 'to know', but in the second clause, 'ye should have known my Father also', the emphasis is upon the Father. They had not recognized Him as the one who was revealing the Father; they only knew Him as the Messiah.

The word here is not 'hereafter' but 'henceforth'. Knowledge and vision, henceforth, would be their spiritual experience because the crisis had come, and He had made Himself known to them as the revealer of the Father.

'Philip saith unto him, Lord, shew us the Father, and it sufficeth us', v. 8

In verses 8 to 14, the emphasis is upon the Father. Verse 9, 'he that hath seen me hath seen the Father'. Verse 10, 'I am in the Father, and the Father in me'. Verse 10, 'the Father that dwelleth in me'. Verse 12, 'I go unto my Father'. Verse 13, 'that the Father may be glorified in the Son'.

Over these verses may be put the heading 'faith'. In verse 10, the word is 'believest'; in verse 11, 'believe me'; in verse 12, 'believeth on me'. These are different statements that all have to do with faith.

The Lord's dialogue with Philip is found in verses 8 to 10. This is the fourth and last appearance of Philip in this Gospel. Thomas could only think of Jesus going to a material place, whereas Philip could only think in terms of a physical sight of the Father, a theophany. Perhaps he was thinking that if Moses, in Exodus chapter 33, saw the Father, surely the Lord could show them the Father. Philip's request deeply affected the Son of God, v. 9. In this connection it is interesting to observe that Philip is the only one in these dialogues whom the Lord addresses by name.

'Show us' is significant. 'Show', *deiknuō*, has the idea of pointing out with the finger and is the same word that is used in Matthew chapter 4 verse 8 in connection with the devil shewing the Lord all the kingdoms of this world and the glory of them. Philip is really saying to the Lord that all that they are asking for is that He would shew them the Father; this would suffice them. In response, in verse 9, there is a mild rebuke for Philip.

'Jesus saith unto him, Have I been so long time with you, and yet hast thou not known me, Philip? he that hath seen me hath seen the Father; and how sayest thou then, Shew us the Father?' v. 9

Philip was one of the first to be called by the Lord in chapter 1, which is why He says, 'Have I been so long time with you', as compared to the others. One can sense deep pathos in the two questions that the Son addresses to Philip. 'Hast not thou known Me?' indicates that Philip had not even recognized Him.

Then He asks, 'how sayest thou then, Shew us the Father?' 'Thou' is emphatic, the significance being, 'thou, Philip'. This is Philip, who from the first responded to His command in chapter 1 to 'follow me'. This is Philip, who pointed out the Lord in chapter 1 verse 45 and spoke of the fulfilment of the scriptures in Him when he said, 'We have found him, of whom Moses in the law, and the prophets, did write'. This is Philip, who also said to Nathaniel, 'Come and see'. Amazingly, He had been so long time with Him and yet he had not known Him. The truth had not dawned on him that Jesus was the revealer of the Father. Had Philip recognized Christ he would never have asked for a theophany. This would have been a limited revelation of God, whereas the Son was the full revelation of the Father. In chapter 17 verse 6, He says to the Father, 'I have manifested thy name unto the men which thou gavest me out of the world'.

'Believest thou not that I am in the Father, and the Father in me? the words that I speak unto you I speak not of myself: but the Father that dwelleth in me, he doeth the works', v. 10

The Lord's reply to Philip is threefold. First, 'I am in the Father, and the Father in me'. Then, second, He refers to the 'words that I speak'. And, third, the 'works that I do', v. 12.

'Believest thou not' seems to imply that Philip might not have believed this truth, though the Lord had already taught it.

In saying, 'I am in the Father, and the Father in me', He is not speaking in terms of equality in the Godhead, though that is involved, but He is speaking of Himself here as a man. This is because He says the Father 'dwelleth in me' and then He goes on to speak about His words and His works. The fact that He says, in verse 12, 'the works that I do shall he', the believer, 'do also', indicates that He is not here speaking of His deity. He is, in fact, speaking in terms of identity and communion rather than in terms of equality in the Godhead.

The Father gave Him the words; and He makes the simple statement that 'the Father . . . doeth the works'. His works were evidently divine. In chapter 10 verses 37 and 38, He says to the Jews, 'If I do not the works of my Father, believe me not. But if I do, though ye believe not me, believe the works: that ye may know, and believe, that the Father is in me, and I in him'. Again, in chapter 14 verse 20, He says, 'At that day ye shall know that I am in my Father, and ye in me, and I in you'. Notice He is speaking of 'that day', the day when the Son would be in heaven and the Spirit on earth. By the Holy Spirit they would know, as we do, that He is in the Father's love and affection, that we are in His

59

love and affection and He is in our love and affection also. A similar though slightly different thought is expressed at chapter 17 verse 21.

'Believe me that I am in the Father, and the Father in me: or else believe me for the very works' sake', v. 11

The verb 'believe' is in the plural, which makes it clear that He is no longer addressing Philip personally but all the disciples. He does this from verses 11 to 21. As He addresses Himself to the disciples, He makes it clear that there are certain things that they should do and there are certain things He would do for them. There were three things that they should do: in verse 11, 'believe me'; in verse 12, 'believe on me'; and, in verses 15 and 21, 'love me'. The things that He would do for them are as follows: in verses 13 and 14, 'whatsoever ye shall ask in my name, that will I do'; in verse 16, 'I will pray the Father'; in verse 18, 'I will come to you'; in verse 21, 'I will love him'; and, in verse 21, I 'will manifest myself'.

When, in verse 11, He says 'believe me', He simply means 'accept my statement' that I am in the Father and the Father in Me. What He seems to be saying is that if His life, His person, His works and the words that He had spoken did not appeal to faith in Him then just take the ground of the enlightened Jews; in chapter 10 verses 37 and 38, He said to the Jews, 'If I do not the works of my Father, believe me not. But if I do, though ye believe not me, believe the works: that ye may know, and believe, that the Father is in me, and I in him'. Again, He said to the Jews in chapter 5 verse 36, 'But I have greater witness than that of John: for the works which the Father hath given me to finish, the same works that I do, bear witness of me, that the Father hath sent me'. It was the works that were bearing witness of Him. This is the ground on which Nicodemus had stood.

'Verily, verily, I say unto you, He that believeth on me, the works that I do shall he do also; and greater works than these shall he do; because I go unto my Father', v. 12

'Verily, verily' indicates that He is introducing a new subject. He is speaking of the works that they who believe in Him would do, because He would go to the Father.

There is no reference to them speaking 'greater words', or even speaking 'His words', but they would do 'greater works'. The works, not His words, would be perpetuated by them. Earlier in the gospel, He said, 'the words that I speak unto you, they are spirit, and they are life', 6. 63; and Simon Peter affirmed, 'thou hast the words of eternal life', 6. 68. These words of eternal life that He spoke belonged exclusively to Him, the Son, but His works are perpetuated.

The works they would do were not greater in degree; no spiritual person would ever compare works in terms of degree. Also, it is not numerically greater works. Rather, the idea is that they would be greater in scope and from the standpoint of mere men doing what Christ did. They would do greater works in scope, 'because I go unto my Father'. His going would increase the sphere of the works. When He was here, His works were confined to the locality where He was, but now that He has gone to the Father, He has sent the Spirit down, who indwells the believers throughout the world. The works have far greater scope, therefore.

The next verse makes very clear that this belongs, strictly speaking, to the pentecostal saints, the early church. This was unique, as we shall see; certain expressions are found here that do not occur anywhere else. It has to do with His going to the Father and what would immediately take place on the earth.

'And whatsoever ye shall ask in my name, that will I do, that the Father may be glorified in the Son', v. 13

It is through prayer that the power of verse 12 would become available. This is the first occurrence of us praying in His name in John's Gospel. It occurs later in chapter 15 verse 16 and chapter 16 verses 23, 24 and 26. There have already been references to His name. He had spoken of believing on His name, 1. 12, and 'many believed in his name', 2. 23. In chapter 3 verse 18, they who have not believed 'in the name of the only

61

begotten Son of God' are condemned already. Believing in His name carries the thought of the name as a seal to a finished work or a completed contract. Then, in chapter 5 verse 43, He says, 'I am come in my Father's name' and He refers, in chapter 10 verse 25, to 'the works that I do in my Father's name'. In chapter 12 verse 13, they say, 'Blessed is the King of Israel that cometh in the name of the Lord'.

Asking 'in my name' is not a mere formula. The first thought is that asking in His name implies that He is absent. Anything done in someone's name implies the absence of that person. Further, anyone doing something in another's name does it as their representative. Therefore, in connection with asking in His name, the Lord gave to the disciples the right of acting on the earth as His representatives, involving asking in the same spirit as He would have done had He been here. When He told the disciples to ask in His name, He was giving to them the same place on the earth that He had before the Father. In prayer, therefore, we have the Son's place before the Father. These are very important matters, not commonly understood.

In Matthew chapter 6 verse 9, He instructed His disciples to pray after this fashion, 'Our Father which art in heaven'. This is not the language of a Christian to be used in God's family today. 'Our Father which art in heaven' is the language of a minor, not the language of one who has entered into his majority and into the truth of sonship. The language of an earthly people, who are the salt of the earth and the light of the world, is 'Our Father which art in heaven'; but the language of this day of grace is, 'our Father' and asking in His Name.

'That will I do', because asking in His name involves conformity to Christ and to the will of Christ, and asking as His representative. The Son will do this so that the Father may be glorified in the Son.

In chapter 15 verse 16, He says, 'Ye have not chosen me, but I have chosen you, and ordained you, that ye should go and bring forth fruit, and that your fruit should remain: that whatsoever ye shall ask of the Father in my name, he may give it you'. He teaches them there that in asking in His name the Father would give it them. Again, He says, 'And in that day ye shall ask me nothing. Verily, verily, I say unto you,

Whatsoever ye shall ask the Father in my name, He will give it you', 16. 23. After John chapter 14, when the Son speaks of asking in His name, He says the Father will give it you, but, in this verse, it is different, because He says that He, the Son, would do it. This is because this verse has to do with the disciples, the pentecostal saints, and has to do with the Son going back to the Father. They are asking in His name and He will do the works; He will perpetuate the greater works in those early disciples. After this, it was the Father who would act. Thus, we have in this verse, and in the earlier chapter, what belongs to the early saints. Again, this is not commonly understood, but it is very important.

The end in view is not that that the Father may be glorified in the disciples who do the works, but 'that the Father may be glorified in the Son'. The greater works were to be done; the power for them comes from asking in His name and the result is that the Father might be glorified in the Son.

'If ye shall ask any thing in my name, I will do it', v. 14

The Revised Version rendering is, 'If ye shall ask me anything in my name, that will I do'. The difference between verses 13 and 14 is that whereas He says, 'whatsoever' in the earlier verse, in the later verse it is asking 'any thing'. Verse 14 is a broader assurance, though in both verses He says He will do it. The 'I' is emphatic, the pledge of the Lord's personal interest and action in relation to His disciples.

If we accept the King James Version, then it is prayer to the Father granted by the Son. If we accept the Revised Version rendering, it is prayer to the Son in His name; that is, praying to the Son and pleading His office.

'If ye love me, keep my commandments', v. 15

The emphasis in verses 15 to 31 is upon the Holy Spirit. He is designated in a threefold way, as the 'Comforter', v. 16, the 'Spirit of truth', v. 17 and the 'Holy Spirit', v. 26 RV. Two thoughts are further stated in connection with the Holy Spirit: He is 'given', v. 16; and He is 'sent', v. 26.

Over these verses may be put the heading 'love', there being references to it in verses 15, 21, 23, 24, 28, and 31. Therefore, we have brought before us hope, vv. 1-3, faith, vv. 4-14, and love, vv. 15-31.

The Revised Version rendering here is, 'If ye love me, ye will keep my commandments'. Up to this point the emphasis has been on the love of the Lord for His disciples, but, for the first time, He now speaks of the disciples' love for their Lord. In chapter 8 verse 42, He said to the Jews, 'If God were your Father, ye would love me'. Now, after His departure, these disciples would no longer be able to minister to the Lord, but they could prove their love to Him by their obedience. 'Keep' is not really an imperative but 'if you love me, you will keep', the thought being that obedience is the obvious and necessary consequence of love.

In 'my commandments', 'my' is emphatic; it involves divine authority.

'And I will pray the Father, and he shall give you another Comforter, that he may abide with you for ever', v. 16

The connection between verses 15 and 16 is simply that they were to look after His interests on the earth by keeping His commandments, v. 15, and He would look after their interests in heaven, v. 16, in praying the Father to give them another Comforter. However, the one is not dependent upon the other.

'Pray' is a different word from the one employed in verses 13 and 14. Here, it is not praying as a suppliant but as an equal. This is the word that is always used of the Son of God, except in one instance. Martha said, in chapter 11 verse 22, 'But I know, that even now, whatsoever thou wilt ask of God, God will give it thee'. She probably did not understand what she was saying, as she used a word concerning the Saviour as a suppliant that is never otherwise used. He never asks as a suppliant but always as one who is on equal terms with the Father.

This verse proves the point that in its context what the Lord is speaking of here has particularly to do with His disciples then present, and the pentecostal saints. He prayed the Father to give them another Comforter on the day of Pentecost; He does not do that for us today

64

because the Comforter has already been given. The moment we believed we received the Holy Spirit, Eph. 1. 13, 14. Now, we ought not to pray for a fresh outpouring of the Spirit, for the Holy Spirit is as much in the believer, in the church and in the world as He was on the day of Pentecost.

The word for 'Comforter' is *paraklētos*, which is used four times in John's Gospel with regard to the Holy Spirit. The idea in a *paraklētos* is one who is summoned to the side of another, to aid and give counsel. The Lord had been with them for three years during which, if they wanted anything, they could call and ask Him. If they were in trouble, He would help them. Now, however, He was going to leave them, but the Father would give them another Comforter, an advocate; He would be in their hearts, and to Him they would have recourse. The Comforter would not take the Lord's place; He would not be instead of Him but in addition to Him. The Spirit counsels, helps, comforts and pleads, and is in addition to Christ, who remains on the throne looking after our interests.

There are two Greek words for the word 'other' or 'another'. *Heteros* means 'another of a different kind' but *allos*, the word employed here, is 'another of the same sort'. The Comforter would, therefore, be another like Himself, of equal status, yet different in that He would 'abide with you for ever'. The Lord had been with them only for a brief season but this other Comforter, whom the Father would give, would never leave them. As long as they are here, He will be here, abiding with them for ever.

In John chapter 20 verse 22, the Lord breathed on them and said unto them, 'Receive ye the Holy Ghost'. In fact, the definite article is omitted, and it should thus read, 'Receive ye holy spirit'. He did not breathe into them the Holy Spirit but, rather, His own risen life. In 1 Corinthians chapter 15 verse 45, reference is made to the last Adam as 'a life-giving spirit' RV. In Genesis chapter 2, God breathed into man the breath of natural life, but, in John chapter 20, the risen Lord breathed into them His own risen life, which can only be enjoyed and experienced in the power of the Spirit, who was given at Pentecost. This is why Romans chapter 8 verse 2 speaks of 'the law of the Spirit of life in Christ Jesus';

the power of the Spirit cannot be divorced from life in Christ Jesus. In John chapter 20, there was an interim in-breathing of the power of the Spirit until the day of Pentecost, when He asked the Father and another Comforter was given. John chapter 7 verse 39 makes it clear that the Holy Spirit would not be given personally until Jesus was glorified.

In John chapter 4 verse 14, the Lord spoke of what would happen in this day of grace, when He said that the water that He would give 'shall be in him a well of water springing up into everlasting life'.

'Even the Spirit of truth; whom the world cannot receive, because it seeth him not, neither knoweth him: but ye know him; for he dwelleth with you, and shall be in you', v. 17

Jesus said in verse 6 that He is 'the truth'; He objectively set forth the truth. 'The Spirit of truth' has brought to us an apprehension of what was made known in Christ, being the conveyor of the truth that was presented objectively in Christ and bearing the truth to man's spirit.

The three different Greek prepositions that are employed here should be observed. In verse 16, 'abide **with** you' is *meta*; in verse 17, 'He dwelleth **with** you' is *para*, which means 'along with'; in verse 17 again, 'and shall be **in** you' is *en*.

'The world cannot receive' the Spirit because it 'seeth him not'; it neither beholds Him nor comes to know Him. The world will only receive what it sees and knows, but the Spirit of truth cannot be seen and known intellectually and therefore the world cannot receive Him. Hence, the world today speaks of the Spirit as being a mere influence.

The charismatic movement embraces people who are not Christians; cultists and Roman Catholics are speaking in tongues, claiming to have the Spirit. People in the charismatic movement say that the scripture says that He will pour out the Spirit on all flesh, including the unconverted, but the Lord here says, 'whom the world cannot receive'. All flesh cannot receive the Holy Spirit today. The 'all flesh' of Joel chapter 2, referred to in Acts chapter 2, would be all flesh who have been born again, entering into the kingdom. It is blasphemous to say the Holy Spirit is operating in this way today on unconverted people, who deny the deity of Christ, know nothing of the new birth and speak in terms of purgatory.

'Ye know him' because He was manifested in Christ.

Today, we enjoy the Holy Spirit abiding with us. The present tense, 'he dwelleth with you', relates to the Comforter dwelling along with these disciples at that time; but He would 'be in you', after the Lord had gone to the Father. What is true of the Spirit today is that He abides with us collectively, v. 16, and is in us individually, v. 17. What the disciples enjoyed when the Lord was present was rather different; then, the Spirit was dwelling alongside them in the person of Christ.

Paul develops these truths in his Epistles. He states that we have the Holy Spirit in us individually, for 1 Corinthians chapter 6 verse 19 says, 'know ye not that your body is the temple of the Holy Ghost which is in you'. The Holy Spirit is also in us collectively, for 1 Corinthians chapter 3 verse 16 says, 'Know ye not that ye are the temple of God, and that the Spirit of God dwelleth in you?' We enjoy the Holy Spirit in this two-fold way: our body is His temple; and the local church is His temple.

The apostle also speaks of grieving the Spirit, Eph. 4. 30, and of quenching the Spirit, 1 Thess. 5. 19. Grieving the Spirit is individual, whereas quenching the Spirit is collective. One way which we may grieve Him is by the kind of language and conversation in which we indulge. 'Let no corrupt communication proceed out of your mouth', Eph. 4. 29. In 1 Thessalonians chapter 5, if any gift is despised in any assembly, the Spirit of God is quenched in His movements in that assembly. Accordingly, He is quenched collectively. These are very important matters to remember.

The teaching regarding the Spirit in John's Gospel is most interesting. In chapter 1 verse 33, John the Baptist says of the Lamb of God, 'the same is he which baptizeth with the Holy Ghost'. In chapter 7 verses 38 and 39, there is the figure of the living water, 'He that believeth on me, as the scripture hath said, out of his belly shall flow rivers of living water. (But this spake he of the Spirit, which they that believe on him

67

should receive: for the Holy Ghost was not yet given; because that Jesus was not yet glorified)'. In chapter 14, however, Jesus is about to be glorified and He tells the disciples of the actual coming of the Comforter, the Holy Spirit.

'I will not leave you comfortless: I will come to you', v. 18

'I will not leave you comfortless' is 'I will not leave you orphans'. In chapter 13 verse 33, the Lord addressed them as 'little children' and, now that He was to leave them, He said that He would not leave them orphans. The only other occurrence of this word in the New Testament is in James chapter 1 verse 27, where it is translated 'fatherless'. In chapter 10 verse 12, He had told them that it is the hireling who leaves the sheep. God's Son was no hireling and He would not leave them. It is true that they would leave Him alone, 16. 32, but He would not leave them comfortless.

The tense employed in 'I will come to you' may be expressed as 'I am coming to you'. This is not a reference to the rapture, such as we have in verse 3 of this chapter, but He is indicating that He is coming to them through the Comforter. It was by the gift of the Holy Spirit that He would come to them. This happened on the day of Pentecost. We are 'an habitation of God through the Spirit', Eph. 2. 22. Thus, Christ comes to us today by the Comforter, the Holy Spirit.

This chapter goes on to teach, in verse 23, that the Father and the Son would make their abode with them, which they do by the Spirit. It is a tremendous truth that we are indwelt by the Godhead! What dignity, therefore, ought to characterize God's people. Perhaps we do not value these things as we should.

'Yet a little while, and the world seeth me no more; but ye see me: because I live, ye shall live also', v. 19

The Lord Jesus now mentions matters in connection with these disciples that are most precious. In verse 19, 'ye see'; in verse 19 again, 'ye ... live'; in verse 20, 'ye ... know'. This was their portion.

'A little while' is found in eight verses in John's Gospel. Though the world would behold Him no more, His own would see Him. When He had passed out of their sight, they would behold Him in the power of the Spirit, as we do. As far as God's Son is concerned, He would, to the world, become just a memory, nothing more than a historical personage. However, His people would continue to behold Him by the Spirit, and this is our portion still.

In chapter 16 verses 20 and 21, He taught them that their sorrow would be turned into joy. This had an immediate fulfilment in chapter 20 verse 20, when the disciples were glad when they saw the Lord. It did not stop there, however, for they continued to behold Him by the Spirit. Just as they were glad when they saw Him in that upper room, so it is still a joy to behold Him today, by the Spirit. 'We see Jesus . . . crowned with glory and honour', Heb. 2. 9.

In saying 'because I live, ye shall live also', He is referring here to His risen life and not to the life that characterized Him here on earth. 'Ye shall' is the future tense and again is to do with Pentecost. They would live in the fullness of resurrection life and power because of His resurrection. This is, then, primarily the life that we live now but, in a secondary sense, this will never cease, for death can never touch it. Because He lives, we live and can never perish.

By way of contrast, the world cannot see, because it is spiritually blind to the glories of Christ. The world beholds Him no more. Unregenerate men and women have no appreciation of the glories of Christ; that lovely man means nothing to them because they are blind to spiritual reality. They do not live, for they are dead in trespasses and sins. They do not know, for they are ignorant of God. They are blind, for they cannot see the glories of Christ. Yet, by grace, all who have been born again have Christ in glory as the object of their heart. We see Him by faith and in the power of the Spirit. We have joy and delight in Christ, and we have the knowledge of the place that we have in His love. We see, we live, and we know things that the world knows nothing about. Let us be encouraged to go in for these things more and more, to live in such a way day by day that these things might not be just a matter of doctrine or theology but that every hour of every day they might be the spiritual enjoyment of the soul.

'At that day ye shall know that I am in my Father, and ye in me, and I in you', v. 20

'At that day' refers to Pentecost and thereafter and so this verse speaks of unique privileges connected with this present day. The expression occurs again at chapter 16 verses 23 and 26. At that day the disciples would know that He is in 'my Father', and they 'in me', and He 'in you'.

It is important to notice the different Greek words used for 'to know'. The word that is employed here, *ginōskō*, means 'you shall come to know by experience'. This experience would be begotten and enjoyed because of the presence of the Comforter, to whose teaching they would submit and whose indwelling power they would know in an increasing manner. This is to be enjoyed by every child of God by reason of the indwelling Spirit. It is not dependent upon external teaching but is something to be personally enjoyed.

In verse 10, He said, 'Believest thou not that I am in the Father, and the Father in me?' Again, in verse 11, He said, 'Believe me that I am in the Father, and the Father in me'. However, it is rather different here in verse 20, which refers to 'that day', the day in which the Holy Spirit is given. Notice also that here He says, 'ye shall know' whereas verses 10 and 11 are to do with what they believe. They would know by experience, by the Holy Spirit, rather than as a matter of faith 'that I am in my Father, and ye in me, and I in you'. These are beautiful expressions.

These disciples, with their Jewish background, were looking for a Messiah who would be enthroned on earth, reigning in glory; they were not looking for one who would be rejected. As against this, the Son of God now tells them that they shall know in the day of the Spirit that 'I am in my Father'. He would be in heaven but even though still here on earth they would have the supreme place in His love and affection, as they would be 'in me'. He also says, 'and I in you', indicating that Christ in heaven would have the supreme place in their (and our) love and affection. What a day this is in which we live, when, by the Spirit, we ought to know experientially that we have one in heaven who has the supreme place in His Father's love, that we have the supreme place in the Son's love and that the Son has the supreme place in our love.

Verse 10 adds, 'and the Father in me' but that is not recorded here for the simple reason that He is now speaking of the portion of the disciples rather than the portion of the Son and His Father.

There is no thought, either here or elsewhere in the upper room ministry, of the Father not loving us. Our unfaithfulness never makes Him to cease loving us, nor does our fidelity result in Him loving us more. However, our fidelity makes us to enjoy what in fact is true just as our infidelity withdraws us from the enjoyment of it. For many this might be just a matter of doctrine or theology, whereas it should be something which we increasingly enjoy, day by day.

'He that hath my commandments, and keepeth them, he it is that loveth me: and he that loveth me shall be loved of my Father, and I will love him, and will manifest myself to him', v. 21

The words 'hath' and 'keepeth' must be observed. 'Hath' is more than just having the Bible. These are two different things and they should never be in conflict.

'My commandments' contain directions for life, every step of the pathway. 'My word', 14. 23 RV, has to do with divine counsel, divine purpose as a whole. 'My words', 12. 48, refers to that divine counsel, as a whole, broken down into its various sections and portions.

The commandments in an old economy were until Christ. That is, the commandments in that day were to show man his sinfulness, to make sin to become transgression and to show man his absolute need of Christ. However, 'my commandments' involve Christ in heaven and the Spirit indwelling us, giving to us the power and energy to keep them, something unknown in the Old Testament.

The third person pronoun 'he' is now used, whereas from verses 18 to 20 the second person pronoun 'ye' is employed. In verses 18 to 20, there is truth in a general way associated with the coming of the Holy Spirit, the Comforter, but in verses 21 to 24 the Lord is speaking of those conditions in which those privileges are to be enjoyed. It is because of this that the teaching is now strictly individual. Notice: in verse 21, 'he'; in verse 23, 'a man'; in verse 24, 'he'. The two conditions in which these privileges are to be enjoyed are love and obedience. If these privileges are not as real to us as they ought to be, the reason could be a lack of love and obedience.

In verse 15, He said 'If ye love me, keep my commandments'. In this verse it is rather different, 'He that hath my commandments, and keepeth them, he it is that loveth me'. We observed that verse 15 should read, 'If ye love me, ye will keep my commandments', the thought being that obedience is the necessary consequence of love. Here, however, it is stating that obedience is the proof of love. Obedience to God's word and to Christ's commandments is not optional.

'Shall be loved of my father' is in the passive form, indicating that it is the conscious knowledge, or the conscious experience, of His love that is in view. He who loves the Son shall feel the love of the Father in his own heart and soul. This gives us to appreciate what the Father thinks of His Son.

Being 'loved of my Father' is not exactly the same as in John chapter 3 verse 16. The Bible speaks of the love of God, the love of the Father, the love of the Son and the love of Christ. These all need to be distinguished. The love of God is always towards the world. The love of the Father is always towards his children. The love of the Son is towards the individual. Usually, the love of Christ is towards His church.

'And I will love him' makes us conscious of the love of divine persons. Not only so, but, He says, I 'will manifest myself to him'. Here, then, is a twofold promise, involving not only being loved but also enlightened. He would present Himself, the glories of His person, in a clear and conspicuous form. Having the Spirit, there would be revealed to them many things about the glorious person of Christ that they did not understand when they were accompanying Him here on earth.

The Spirit of God causes us, too, to behold His glory. In fact, this idea of beholding His glory is continually the mind of God for his people. In John chapter 1 verse 14, 'we beheld his glory' is beholding His glory in the past. In 2 Corinthians chapter 3 verse 18, it says, 'we all, with open face beholding as in a glass the glory of the Lord, are changed into the same image from glory to glory, even as by the Spirit of the Lord'. That is beholding the glory of the Lord in the present. In the future, John 17. 24, those whom the Father has given Him shall behold His glory.

'Judas saith unto him, not Iscariot, Lord, how is it that thou wilt manifest thyself unto us, and not unto the world?' v. 22

In verses 23 and 24, the Lord gives a simple answer to the request by Judas as to why He would not manifest Himself to the world. In verse 23, He speaks of His own; in verse 24, He speaks of others who are of the world. The big difference is that in verse 23 His own love Him and they keep His sayings, whereas in verse 24 others do not love Him or keep His sayings.

It has been mentioned in chapter 13 verse 30 that Judas Iscariot had gone out, but John is very careful to ensure that he is not confused with any of the other disciples, especially the Judas about whom he is now speaking.

In asking this question Judas had something in his mind akin to that of our Lord's own brethren after the flesh in chapter 7 verse 4, when they said unto Him, 'If thou do these things, shew thyself to the world'. They could only think in terms of Jesus as being the Messiah. They thought that as Messiah He should be manifesting Himself to the world in judgement upon His own enemies and the enemies of the nation of Israel. The Psalmist had said of Him, 'Ask of me, and I shall give unto thee the heathen for thine inheritance', Ps. 2. 8, and the disciples might have wondered why He was not doing that now to restore the kingdom. They seemed to think that something had taken place to change all this.

Judas' question should read something like this, 'Lord what is come to pass that Thou wilt manifest Thyself unto us and not unto the world?'

The wonderful day is coming, of course, when our Lord shall be manifested to the wondering eyes of men and women in this world. Peter says we shall be 'glad also with exceeding joy' in that day, 1 Pet. 4. 13, but now is not the time for His manifestation to the world. No doubt they had thought that if He would manifest Himself to the world they would, as His disciples, share in such a manifestation. He had in fact already said to them, 'ye which have followed me, in the regeneration when the Son of man shall sit in the throne of his glory, ye also shall sit upon twelve thrones, judging the twelve tribes of Israel', Matt. 19. 28. They knew, then, that they must share in this. Whether that was predominant in their minds or not it had a place, no doubt.

In Luke chapter 19, the Lord uttered the parable concerning the nobleman who went into a far country to receive for himself a kingdom and to return. He spoke this parable because they expected that the kingdom of God would immediately appear. Then, in Acts chapter 1 verse 6, they said to the Lord Jesus, 'Lord, wilt thou at this time restore again the kingdom to Israel?' We are reminded again, therefore, that these questions and interruptions made by the disciples must be understood against the background of their Jewish expectation.

'Jesus answered and said unto him, If a man love me, he will keep my words: and my Father will love him, and we will come unto him, and make our abode with him', v. 23

Strictly speaking, 'words' is in the singular. 'If a man love me he will keep my word'. He tells Judas that it is not a manifestation to the world now, see verse 22, but a question of individuals, and the great matter is loving Him and keeping His word. In verse 15, the language was, 'If ye love me, ye will keep my commandments'. His commandments contain His directions for the disciples in respect of the pathway of discipleship and, if they loved Him, they would keep them. Here, however, it is not His 'commandments' or even His 'words' but His 'word'. This is not simply directions for the pathway; rather, He is referring to an

74

unfolding of divine counsel concerning His Father's will, the purpose of the Father's heart both for the present and for the future. He speaks of keeping such a word, of treasuring it in one's heart.

In salvation, obedience is an evidence of faith, but in the path of discipleship obedience is an evidence of love. Keeping His word is a necessary consequence of loving Him.

Strictly speaking, His word is not His but the Father's which sent Him. Whoever loves the Son and keeps His word is loved by the Father, 'my Father will love Him'. Love of Christ and treasuring His word brings one into the enjoyment of the Father's love.

'We will come . . . and make our abode with him' is rather different to the Messiah manifesting Himself to the world. When, as Messiah, He manifests Himself to the world there is going to be feigned obedience on the part of many because of God's power, but in the present day individuals love Him and in sincerity keep His word. These individuals are loved by the Father, and the Father and the Son make their abode with them, establishing permanent fellowship with them.

As we have seen, failure to keep His word does not cause the Father to cease to love us, but keeping His word keeps us in the enjoyment of the Father's love. There are conditions, therefore, for the enjoyment of the Father's love.

In 1 John chapter 4 verse 15, John writes, 'Whosoever shall confess that Jesus is the Son of God, God dwelleth in him, and he in God'. In that verse the preposition is *en*, 'within', but here it is *para*, 'alongside of'. Here, therefore, it is not so much the thought of dwelling within but of fellowship with divine persons. It is, perhaps, not commonly understood that whether it is 'within' or 'alongside of' this is something that is enjoyed by reason of the person of the Spirit; it is by the Spirit that the Father and the Son abide in, or 'along with', us. He is the Spirit of the Father and He is the Spirit of the Son.

God's purpose from the beginning was to have communion with man. That will yet be realized in the eternal state when 'the tabernacle of

God is with men, and he will dwell with them', Rev. 21. 3. God is not dwelling with men yet but both the Father and the Son by the Spirit abide with us and so we anticipate what shall yet be realized in the eternal state.

'He that loveth me not keepeth not my sayings: and the word which ye hear is not mine, but the Father's which sent me', v. 24

The singular 'word' in verse 23 is the same word here translated 'sayings', though here it is in the plural. Here, then, is the difference between the disciples who love Him, v. 23, and the world, described in the phrase 'He that loveth me not', v. 24. The reason for the Lord Jesus not manifesting Himself to the world is that there were those of the world who did not love Him. When it is the disciple, v. 23, it is the word as a whole that is treasured and kept, but the unbeliever rejects not only the totality of it but also its details. Hence the word is in the plural here. Disobedience involves God; to reject Christ's word is to reject the Father's word. The Son goes on to say, therefore, 'the word which ye hear is not mine, but the Father's which sent me'.

The conclusion of our Lord's upper room ministry, vv. 25-31

These verses are still in the section in which the emphasis is upon the Holy Spirit. In fact, it is only in this section that the full title of 'the Holy Spirit' is given to the Comforter in John's Gospel. In chapter 1 verse 33, chapter 7 verse 39 and chapter 20 verse 22, the definite article is omitted. No doubt there is a significance about that.

In this section the Lord again reverts to the subject of His going away. In verse 25, He speaks of 'being yet present with you' or 'yet abiding with you'. In verse 28, 'Ye have heard how I said unto you, I go away' and, in verse 30, 'the prince of this world cometh'. One can almost feel the sense of crisis in these words of the Lord Jesus. In view of His going away, He is assuring them of an abundant provision for them during the time of His absence and that though He would be absent they would remain the object of divine interest on the earth.

In this section, He makes mention of two things in particular. He tells them of what the Father would send them and He tells them of what He Himself would leave them. The Father would send them the Comforter, v. 26, and the Son would leave them His peace, v. 27. This is most gracious provision.

What He has to say to them now is sad and moving, yet most assuring. He assures them that His gracious ministry, the words that He had been speaking to them, would not be lost.

In this section, He speaks of His past and present ministry and His future provision. He speaks of His **past** ministry in verses 25, 28 and 29. 'These things have I spoken unto you, being yet present with you', v. 25. 'Ye have heard how I said unto you', v. 28. 'I have told you before it come to pass', v. 29. He also speaks of His ministry then **present** with His disciples. He says in verse 30, 'Hereafter I will not talk much with you' or 'I will no more speak much with you'. The word 'hereafter' in the King James Version might suggest that He is thinking in terms of the future, but the thought is rather 'from this moment onward'. This was to be characteristic of His being then present with them, 'from this moment I will no more speak much with you'. With regard to His **future** provision He says, 'But the Comforter, which is the Holy Ghost, whom the Father will send in my name, he shall teach you all things, and bring all things to your remembrance, whatsoever I have said unto you', v. 26. His past ministry would not be lost.

In verses 25 to 29, He is thinking of every situation during the time of His absence and, in wondrous grace, He is making provision for their every need.

In verse 26, He makes **provision for His absence**; the Comforter will be sent in His name. 'His name' involves His absence, but here was one who would represent Him. In verse 27, He makes **provision for their fear**; He says, 'My peace I give unto you' and 'Let not your heart be troubled'. In verse 28, there is **provision for their sadness**; 'If ye loved me, ye would rejoice, because I said, I go unto the Father'. He tells them not to be sad; though He is leaving them He is going to the Father. In verse 29, He makes **provision for their alarm**; 'I have told you before it come to pass'.

In verses 30 and 31, He refers to two matters connected with His imminent death. Verse 30 makes it clear that though He was going to die, death would have no claim upon Him, and, in verse 31, though He would die, His death was voluntary. The prince of this world had nothing in our Saviour and, therefore, death had no claim upon Him. If death had no claim upon Him, He would die voluntarily and so He says, 'Arise, let us go hence', to Golgotha.

'These things have I spoken unto you, being yet present with you', v. 25

He is now introducing another line of thought and teaching. 'These things have I spoken unto you' refers to what He had spoken unto them that particular evening, but in verse 26 there is a contrast, 'the Comforter . . . shall teach you all things'. Notice, then, the difference between verses 25 and 26. In verse 25, 'These things', but in verse 26, 'all things'.

In verse 23, there would be a future abiding with them but here He is speaking of His 'being yet' with them, His present abiding with them in wondrous grace. In verse 26, He says of the Comforter, 'whom the Father will send in my name'. 'In His name' involves His absence, but He is here speaking of being yet present with them.

'But the Comforter, which is the Holy Ghost, whom the Father will send in my name, he shall teach you all things, and bring all things to your remembrance, whatsoever I have said unto you', v. 26

The Comforter would be sent 'in my name', to represent the Son's interests, and 'he shall teach you all things, and bring all things to your remembrance, whatsoever I have said unto you'.

The Father sending in His name is not connected with the Son asking, as in verse 16, but with the Father giving. The idea in verse 16 is that what the Son was to the Father, the Holy Spirit now is to the Son, but

78

now, in verse 26, the Father has sent the Spirit in the name of the Son, to represent the Son's interests. The Father, then, sent the Son in His name to represent the Father's interests; now, the Father has sent the Spirit in the Son's name to represent the Son's interests. As the Son was the Father's representative to make Him known, so now the Holy Spirit is the Son's representative to make Him known to us.

If anything is done in His name it is done when He is absent, not just with His authority but as His representative. When it comes to asking in His name, we are even now given the Son's place before the Father and asking in His name is not, therefore, merely appending the expression 'in His name' at the beginning or end of a prayer. Asking in His name is asking as His representative, having the same place that He has before the Father.

The word 'Comforter' does not really convey the idea of comfort in the sense of solace. He is one who teaches in the sense of an advocate, pleading, arguing, convincing. The Greek word *paraklētos* is a compound of two words, *para* and *kaleō*, meaning 'alongside of' and 'to call'. It describes one who was summoned to the side of another to give aid and is often used as giving aid in a court of justice as the counsel for the defence.

He speaks of the Comforter here as the great teacher who would teach them all things and, in doing so, He emphasizes the moral character of the teacher; He is 'the Holy Spirit'; this is the only mention of that full title. Because 'he shall teach you all things', we have the New Testament Epistles; because He would 'bring all things to your remembrance', we have the Gospels. Because 'he will shew you things to come', 16. 13, we have the book of Revelation. Thus, the whole New Testament is divinely inspired.

John could only remember the words in his Gospel so accurately because of the fulfilment of this promise, though we might apply the principle that the Holy Spirit is our teacher and can bring things to our remembrance. To know that nothing that He personally had taught them would be lost must have been precious to the hearts of the apostles here in the upper room.

When the four Gospels are taken together, the narrative only comprehends but a few days of our Lord's public ministry. John chapter 21 verse 25 tells us that 'there are also many other things which Jesus did, the which, if they should be written every one, I suppose that even the world itself could not contain the books that should be written'. The statement, that He would 'bring all things to your remembrance, whatsoever I have said unto' you, is very important. The recollection and repetition of the words that the Lord spoke was not left to the memory of the apostles. The Gospels are not the product of the uncertain recollection of these particular sermons. These belonged to divine inspiration, the Spirit bringing to their remembrance whatsoever the Lord had said unto them.

All scripture is given by inspiration of God; it is God-breathed. In 1 Timothy chapter 5 verse 18, it says, 'For the scripture saith, Thou shalt not muzzle the ox that treadeth out the corn. And, The labourer is worthy of his reward'. Both are termed 'the scripture'. It is in Deuteronomy chapter 25 verse 4 that the scripture says, 'Thou shalt not muzzle the ox', but the second quotation is from Luke chapter 10 verse 7. This, therefore, is also viewed as scripture. The writings of Paul are also termed 'scriptures', in 2 Peter chapter 3 verses 15 and 16. 'Our beloved brother Paul also according to the wisdom given unto him hath written unto you; as also in all his epistles, speaking in them of these things; in which are some things hard to be understood, which they that are unlearned and unstable wrest, as they do also the other scriptures, unto their own destruction'.

Applying the principle, the Spirit of God at the appropriate time will bring to our remembrance the scriptures we have read, as necessary, for the blessing of ourselves and others. It must be remembered, though, that Paul says in Colossians chapter 3 verse 16, 'Let the word of Christ dwell in you richly'. It is only as the word of Christ dwells in us richly that the Spirit of God has something to work on.

'He shall teach you all things' indicates that they would have the personality of the Holy Spirit. In fact, the pronoun 'He' is emphatic. In verse 25, He speaks of 'these things' but in verse 26 it is 'all things'. In chapter 16 verse 12, the Son says, 'I have yet many things to say unto you, but ye cannot bear them now'; they did not have the spiritual capacity to grasp them. The Lord Jesus found it necessary to put a limit upon His teaching and therefore it was just 'these things'. The Comforter, however, would capacitate them for comprehensive teaching and so He now speaks of 'all things'.

The truth of 1 Corinthians chapter 2 verse 13, 'Which things also we speak, not in the words which man's wisdom teacheth, but which the Holy Ghost teacheth; comparing spiritual things with spiritual', is very much akin to the teaching here. 1 Corinthians chapter 2 is apostolic in its character, 'we have the mind of Christ', v. 16. The apostles had the intelligence of Christ and the words which they spoke were the words which the Holy Spirit gave. No servant could claim that today. This was divine inspiration in the apostolic ministry.

He is our teacher, too, but here it is strictly apostolic. Nothing has to be added to apostolic revelation as it is complete. Even Timothy had to restate what he had been taught. Paul, of course, comes in as a unique vessel, as an apostle of Christ Jesus. In Galatians chapter 1 verse 16 Paul speaks of the fact that it pleased God 'to reveal his Son in me'. That was not said of anyone else, including the twelve. It is not revealing the Son **to** Paul, or even **through** Paul, but because Paul was not one of the twelve, the Father revealed the Son **in** him. There was a special in-shining into Paul of the Son of God Himself, which was to do with His unique ministry.

'Peace I leave with you, my peace I give unto you: not as the world giveth, give I unto you. Let not your heart be troubled, neither let it be afraid', v. 27

'Peace I leave with you' was a wonderful thing but even more so as He says it is 'my peace'. To some extent, this was His farewell message. 'Shalom' was usually a greeting but it is as if He uses it here as His farewell message. 'My peace' was the peace that He enjoyed when He was here. It was the peace of unbroken communion, beneath an unclouded sky. 'I leave' it as a bequest; 'I give' it so that it will become your possession.

He does not say here that He would remove their trouble from them but that He would give them His peace despite their trouble. This would make them superior to the trouble so that they would not be afraid. Undoubtedly, this has to do with the presence of the Comforter.

Peace can involve bringing a calm out of the storm, but peace can also involve a tranquillity in the midst of the storm. It is interesting to observe that Paul speaks of 'the peace of God', also rendered 'the peace of Christ', Col. 3. 15, where he says, 'And let the peace of God rule in your hearts, to the which also ye are called in one body; and be ye thankful'. The word 'rule' there means 'to arbitrate', to 'act as an umpire'; we are to let the peace of Christ have the last word in our heart in every anxiety and problem, and to be thankful. This is allowing the peace of Christ to take over in my life.

In Romans chapter 5 verse 1, peace **with** God has to do with our conscience; it is in relation to our sins and our eternal security. We are justified; our sins have been dealt with. In Philippians chapter 4 verse 7, the peace **of** God is not connected with our sins but our anxieties, not with our conscience but with our heart and mind. There, the peace of God keeping our heart and mind through Christ Jesus is not connected with our eternal security but with God's daily provision for our minds. The peace of Christ is the peace of uninterrupted communion with the Father, the peace that Christ Himself enjoyed when He was here.

He gives, 'not as the world giveth'. The world generally gives what it cannot keep and leaves what it cannot take, but our Lord here gives what He could have kept. Also, He not only gives but also retains this peace, so that this is a peace that we share with Him. He is not describing what He gives but how He gives, and how differently the world gives.

The opening verse in the chapter is, in essence, repeated here. 'Let not your heart be troubled, neither let it be afraid' is the realization of His peace not through the removal of the trouble but despite it and in the midst of it. Years ago, there was an art competition where artists were invited to paint a depiction of peace. The many paintings offered for the competition were generally quiet, tranquil country scenes but the painting that won was of a little bird happily resting on a ledge while the waterfall was falling in a torrent round about it. That is peace in the midst of trouble.

In Luke chapter 2 verse 14, the angelic host said, 'Glory to God in the highest, and on earth peace, good will toward men'. But, in Luke chapter 12 verse 51, He said, 'Suppose ye that I am come to give peace on earth? I tell you, Nay; but rather division'. He came to bring peace, but the result was not peace but a sword, because they were divided concerning Him. Had they all received Him they would have had peace in their heart, but they were divided, and the result was the sword.

'Ye have heard how I said unto you, I go away, and come again unto you. If ye loved me, ye would rejoice, because I said, I go unto the Father: for my Father is greater than I', v. 28

The Lord refers to what He had said in verses 2 to 4. In saying 'If ye loved me', He means 'If ye loved me with an unselfish love'. If their thoughts were not so much on their loss but, rather, on His gain they would rejoice. In thinking of His going in terms of their loss, they were made sad, but if they loved Him unselfishly, they would think of His gain, in that He was going to the Father. This would cause them to rejoice. In verse 27, then, it is peace for a fearful heart, but in verse 28 it is joy for an unselfish heart.

It is important to note that it is not 'my Father' but 'the Father'. He is going back as man to the Father who had sent Him on a mission, which was now accomplished, and who had given Him a work, which was now finished.

In 'for my Father is greater than I', it is, again, literally 'the Father'. The Father is not greater than the Son as to His person, for they are equal, but the Son speaks of the Father as greater in the sense of His mission as the sent one; it was the Father who had sent Him. That is why He is emphasizing He is going back to 'the Father'.

'And now I have told you before it come to pass, that, when it is come to pass, ye might believe', v. 29

'And now' is important. At this vital moment when the crisis of His departure is upon them, He told them so that in this 'ye might believe'. This is not as in chapter 13 verse 19, 'Now I tell you before it come, that, when it is come to pass, ye may believe that I am he', which is His deity. Here, the thought is 'that . . . ye might believe me' in the sense of having Him in glory as an object of faith.

'Hereafter I will not talk much with you: for the prince of this world cometh, and hath nothing in me', v. 30

'Hereafter' is 'from this point onwards'. The crisis had come. He was thinking of His death, which is why the enemy, the prince of this world which had rejected Him, was coming. He had a work to do and the enemy, was approaching. After His temptation, the devil departed for a season and now he comes. It was for this reason that He would not now talk much with them.

There are three references in John's Gospel to the devil as the ruler, or prince, of this world, the one who exercises dominion or authority over it. In chapter 12 verse 31, the Saviour said, 'Now is the judgment of this world: now shall the prince of this world be cast out'; and in chapter 16 verse 11, He says, 'Of judgment, because the prince of this world is judged'. The teaching of chapter 12 verse 31 is that the world was judged in its prince; he instigated our Lord's condemnation by the world and the world was judged in its ruler, its prince. Now he is the 'god of this age' or the 'god of this world', 2 Cor. 4. 4. Calvary has constituted the devil the god of an impenitent age.

'Hath nothing in me' means that there was nothing in our Lord over which, as a ruler, the prince of this world could exercise his power, particularly as the one who had the power of death.

'But that the world may know that I love the Father; and as the Father gave me commandment, even so I do. Arise, let us go hence', v. 31

In John chapter 17 verse 23, He speaks of a coming day when He will share His glory with us, so that the world will know that the Father sent Him and that the Father loved us as He loved Him. Here, however, it is something rather different. It is 'that the world may know that I love the Father; and as the Father gave me commandment, even so I do'. The world would come to know through the preaching of the gospel that His death was voluntary, being out of love to the Father.

He has been teaching His own that obedience is the proof of love. Here is the proof that the Lord was the great example of His own ministry. 'As the Father gave me commandment, even so I do'.

When He says, 'Arise, let us go hence', they leave the upper room. Some suggest that there was some delay, but John would surely have observed this. It is the same as in Matthew chapter 26 verse 46, 'Rise, let us be going: behold, he is at hand that doth betray me'. Jesus went forth with His disciples into the garden in chapter 18 verse 1. This is not the going forth from the upper room but the going forth from the city. Here, it is going forth from the upper room that He might go voluntarily to Golgotha in obedience to the Father and out of love to Him. John writes from this particular standpoint; Christ goes into death in obedience to, and out of love for, the Father.

Chapter 15

In the last verse of chapter 14, the Saviour said to His disciples, 'But that the world may know that I love the Father; and as the Father gave me commandment, even so I do. Arise, let us go hence'. With these words our Saviour leaves the upper room with His disciples and these, His own, find themselves in the outside world.

In chapter 13, John's feet are in Jesus' hands and his head is on Jesus' bosom, directing attention to two important matters in connection with the upper room, namely cleansing and communion. In chapter 14, there are two important matters in connection with the Son, namely the announcement of the Son coming **for** His own and, in the meantime, He would come **to** them. In chapter 15 and in subsequent chapters, not now in the upper room but in the outside world, the Lord is teaching them their twofold responsibility to the Father and to the Son, in that world. Their responsibility to the Father, found in verse 8, was to bring forth fruit for His pleasure. Their responsibility to the Son, found in verse 27, was to bear witness to Him. This is always God's order: the privileges of the upper room, involving cleansing and communion, the enjoyment of the intimacies of the heart of the Father and of the Son, followed by our responsibility in the world.

This chapter can be divided very simply into three sections. In verses 1 to 8, the disciples were taught their responsibility to Christ, which was to abide in Him, vv. 4, 7. In verses 9 to 17, they were taught their responsibility to each other, which was to love one another, vv. 12, 17. In verses 18 to 27, they were taught their responsibility towards the world, which was to bear witness to Him, v. 27.

Another way in which this section can be remembered is that in verses 1 to 8 His own are viewed as His disciples, in verses 9 to 17 they are viewed as His friends and in verses 18 to 27 they are viewed as His witnesses.

In verses 1 to 8, the emphasis is upon the Father. 'My Father is the husbandman', v. 1; 'Herein is my Father glorified', v. 8. In verses 9 to 17, the emphasis is upon the Son who speaks about 'my commandments', v. 10; 'my love', v. 10; 'my joy', v. 11; 'my friends', v. 14; 'my name' v. 16. In verses 18 to 27, the emphasis is upon the Holy Spirit. Verse 26 is a tremendously important verse about the Holy Spirit in which He, the Comforter, 'comes', 'is sent' and 'proceeds'.

The disciples' responsibility to Christ, vv. 1-8

'I am the true vine, and my Father is the husbandman', v. 1

In this section the emphasis is upon the Father and the subject is that of the vine. It is important to note that the Lord is disclosing, predominantly, the setting aside of the nation of Israel. The main thought in connection with the vine is that of fruitfulness. Ezekiel chapter 15 verse 3 shows that nothing can be done with the wood of a vine, not even a pin can be made from it upon which to hang a vessel. The vine is only good for bearing fruit. In the Old Testament scriptures Israel was repeatedly spoken of as a vine. 'Thou hast brought a vine out of Egypt', Ps. 80. 8, is a reference to the nation of Israel. In Isaiah chapter 5, in connection with this vine, the Lord fenced it and gathered out the stones. Here, then, was a vine brought out of Egypt, loved and cared for by God Himself. Jeremiah chapter 2 speaks of Israel as a 'noble vine' which the Lord brought out of Egypt, loved it and cared for it. However, in Isaiah chapter 5 verse 2, this vine brought forth wild grapes and so failed completely in the purpose for which God had brought it out of Egypt. Jeremiah states that this vine had become 'degenerate' and 'strange'. Hosea chapter 10 verse 1 speaks of Israel as an 'empty vine', the conclusive proof of this being their rejection of their Messiah.

Against that background the Lord Jesus now turns to His disciples and says, 'I am the true vine'. He did not mean true in contrast to false but true in the sense that what was partially seen in Israel is perfectly and completely seen in Him. A person was part of that noble vine if a child of Abraham by natural descent and able to call Jacob their father, but that is all finished with now. The Lord seeks to make them understand that this is not now the case. In place of that the Lord says, 'I am the true vine'.

This is very important to understand. It is not possible to properly understand these verses except it be seen that what the Lord is teaching is that both He and His disciples are now taking the place of what Israel was in the Old Testament upon the earth. Christ and His disciples are taking the place of Jerusalem and her children. Thus, when we think of the vine, we do not have before us Christianity in its heavenly character. Many have gone astray in the 'fall away' doctrine because they fail to observe this. Vines are not connected with heaven; they are connected with the earth, Rev. 14. 18. Thus, in John chapter 15, we are not thinking of the church as the body of Christ that has its head in heaven but of a vine that has its roots on the earth. It is the matter of discipleship and disciples in profession.

Let it be clear that there is a vast difference between being 'in Christ' in a Pauline sense and being in the vine. 'In Christ' conveys to our mind the thought of life, security and the blessed truth that there can be no condemnation, but 'in the vine' the thought is of fruitfulness, discipleship and profession.

'Every branch in me that beareth not fruit he taketh away: and every branch that beareth fruit, he purgeth it, that it may bring forth more fruit', v. 2

The emphasis here is clearly upon fruit, as it is in verses 4 and 5. In this verse there is 'no fruit', 'fruit' and 'more fruit' and, in verse 5, 'much fruit'. Fruit is something that must be considered as distinct either from gift or service, otherwise there would be those who would be excluded. Fruit is not to do with the saints of God being helped or souls being saved. Fruit-bearing is like feet-washing in that it belongs to all the saints of God, brother and sister alike. Fruit is character, the reproduction of Christ in the life. This is more important than having the ability to teach the saints or preach the gospel. This might be done with acceptance and yet there be little fruit, in that little of Christ is seen in the life. In fact, it is not always the case that the most gifted are the most Christ-like. It is more desirable to be Christ-like than gifted, for the Father is looking for this fruit in His people. In this, He is not only skilful, but this vine is cherished by Him.

There is a twofold way in which expositors have looked at the expression 'he taketh away'. Some have rendered it as 'lifting up'. However, in New Testament usage the emphasis is always upon being 'taken away' rather than being 'lifted up'. Those who interpret it as being 'lifted up' expound the verse as having the significance that a branch is trailing in the dust or the earth. Fruit is not being produced and so the husbandman lifts it up. It should be observed, however, that the object of this operation is not stated. If it meant being 'lifted up' from the earth it would be stated that the intention would be that it might bear fruit, or more fruit, or much fruit, as is the case later in this verse where He cleanses it in order that there might be more fruit. Whatever the Father does has an object in view with regard to fruit, but here that is not so. It is simply stated, 'He taketh away'. It is not the thought here of 'lifting up', therefore, but of being 'taken away' as a matter of the Father's discipline towards His own. This makes this matter very solemn. If we are not bearing fruit as far as the Father is concerned, if there is not that reproduction of Christ in our life, it would be better that we were not here. Some might argue that the Father is not doing this kind of thing today and, generally speaking, that is true, but never let us forget that the Father always retains that particular right and prerogative to take away branches which are not bearing fruit. There is nothing more important than that Christ should be reproduced in our lives.

This is what we have, for instance, in 1 Corinthians chapter 11 verse 30, 'For this cause many are weak and sickly among you, and many sleep'. There is a progression: weakness first, sickness next, and sleeping last. God wanted His voice to be heard first of all in weakness, but if they refused to hear His voice in weakness God visited them with sickness. Then, if they refused to hear His voice in sickness, God took them away in death. That is how James chapter 5 verses 14 and 15 may be understood. There, a brother who is sick sends for the elders, who anoint him. He confesses his sin, is converted from his ways, and is saved from death. It is because he repents of his sin that he is saved from death. No Christian, or anyone who bears the name of Christ, has any licence or right to live haphazardly, showing a complete disregard as to whether or not they are reproducing Christ in their life.

There are always instances in the life of any disciple when Christ is not being reproduced but it is character that is in view here, where the sum total of their profession is that they are not fruitful. Nobody is marked by sinless perfection, always reproducing Christ, but here is one who is always not reproducing Christ. 'Beareth' is in the present continuous tense.

Paul says in 2 Corinthians chapter 3 verse 3, 'Forasmuch as ye are manifestly declared to be the epistle of Christ'. He does not say 'epistles' of Christ; it is singular, and the reference is to the whole church. The whole assembly ought to be an epistle of Christ, known and read of all men. This happens when individuals in the assembly are reproducing Christ without a blot, without a stain. If it should be that one in the assembly is not reproducing Christ so that Christ is not being seen and read in him, that one is a blot upon that epistle. Not only does it affect the Father but also the world. It is possible that a believer's relationship with next door neighbours, business associates or work colleagues can be of such a sort that there is a blot on what otherwise would be a lovely epistle, a letter of Christ known and read of all men.

The Father is continually looking for more fruit from our lives. Just as the husbandman would free the branch from those useless shoots and leaves which prey upon it and hinder the production of quality fruit, so the Father would cleanse us that there might be more fruit, and quality fruit, in our lives. Cleansing is not necessarily the removal of evil from the life, but it is the removing of everything that does not have Christ for its object. This is not so much to cleanse us from an immoral life, unrighteous feelings, or a lying tongue, for we know these things are wrong, but by the word of the Father He wants us to deal with everything in the life that does not have Christ for its object. That is high ground. How much cleaner would we be in our personal lives, our homes and our businesses if we recognized that the Father would cleanse from our lives everything that does not have Christ as its object. This is in order that there might be more fruit. He does this in the manner described in verse 3.

'Now ye are clean through the word which I have spoken unto you', v. 3

In chapter 13 verses 10 and 11, Judas was present in the upper room when Jesus said, 'And ye are clean, but not all. For he knew who should betray Him'. However, in chapter 15, Judas had gone out and so the Lord says, 'Now ye are clean through the word which I have spoken unto you'. There were now no exceptions, as Judas was absent.

By His word the Father cleanses from the life everything that does not have Christ as its object. That sounds straightforward doctrinally and from the standpoint of good theology, but it is a very practical matter. There is the need to spend time with God's word, reading it with an exercised heart, to hear the Father speaking through His word, pointing out those things in the life that do not have Christ for their object, and to respond and be cleansed. Regrettably, for many of us the Bible has become a neglected book.

'Abide in me, and I in you. As the branch cannot bear fruit of itself, except it abide in the vine; no more can ye, except ye abide in me', v. 4

Much fruit is produced by abiding in the vine. Indeed, it is only by abiding in Him that fruit is produced. 'The branch cannot bear fruit of itself' simply means that no branch has a source of life in itself. There is, therefore, this twofold exhortation, 'Abide in me and I in you'. 'Abide in me' is our responsibility; 'I in you' is the result. As we abide in Him, He is reproduced in us.

To abide in Him is simply to cleave to Christ. This is not just recognizing that we need Him, in that we cannot live without him, and it is much more than knowing him either as a Saviour or the one who helps in all the difficulties and problems of life. Abiding in Him simply means that His incomparable worth has completely won and captivated my heart, the warmth and beauty of His holy person thrilling my whole being. Abiding in Him involves cultivating a continual sense of His presence so that His preciousness means more to me than anything else in this world. Let us not just accept this as doctrine or theology but apply this to our hearts.

Abiding in Him is the means whereby we can be the disciples that we ought to be. This means we have to learn to deal with self; we cannot abide in Him if we are marked by self-confidence or have never got beyond trusting self. Discipleship involves following His example. In John chapter 13, it is following His example in the matter of feet-washing; in 1 Peter chapter 2, it is in the matter of suffering. It means that, no matter what circumstance of life we find ourselves in, the Father looks down and sees in us a reproduction of what His Son would have been and done. Abiding in Him is walking even as He walked. 'He that saith he abideth in him ought himself also so to walk, even as he walked', 1 John 2. 6. In that verse, the word 'ought' means a debt is involved to walk even as He walked.

'I am the vine, ye are the branches: He that abideth in me, and I in him, the same bringeth forth much fruit: for without me ye can do nothing', v. 5

In verse 2, there is 'more fruit' but here there is 'much fruit'. In verse 2, the Father cleanses to produce more fruit, but, in verse 5, it is by abiding in Him that we produce much fruit. That fruit is not so much for the world to see but it is for the heart of the Father.

'Without me ye can do nothing' is sometimes applied to the matter of service but it is really to do with the matter of fruit-bearing. We might have everything in this world that we could desire and yet, with nothing for the Father in the life, there may be little fruit. Another might be deprived of all these things, but Christ is everything to him; the result would be 'much fruit'.

'If a man abide not in me, he is cast forth as a branch, and is withered; and men gather them, and cast them into the fire, and they are burned', v. 6

The statement 'as a branch' means that what is in view here is a branch in profession. To further prove that this is so, notice that at the end of verse 5, when He says, 'For without me ye can do nothing', He uses the second person pronoun 'ye'. Then, in verse 7, He uses it again, referring, of course, in both verses to the disciples to whom He is speaking. In verse 6, however, the language is different. He does not say, 'If ye abide not in me' but 'If a man abide not in me'. If it were 'ye', a genuine disciple could be 'cast forth', but He is speaking of a branch in profession.

Further, notice that He says 'If a man abide not in me', not 'If a man does not bear fruit'. In verse 2, He speaks of branches not bearing fruit, but He does not say this in verse 6, where there is no possibility or question of fruit, for it is a branch in profession. In verse 6, it is not a question of fruit; it is the question of abiding.

Then He says, 'He is cast forth'. It is the word that is used of the man cast out of the synagogue in John chapter 9 verse 34. Notice again the difference from verse 2. There, 'He taketh away' has the thought of being removed in discipline, but, in verse 6, 'He is cast forth', which is the judicial government of God, penal in its character. 'And men gather them, and cast them into the fire, and they are burned' views men as instruments of God's government. In this verse, the Lord Jesus has Judas in mind, a man who did not abide and was cast forth, and, in the governmental dealings of God, men gathered him and burned him. Judas was a branch in profession, cast forth by God because of his treachery. Men were glad to pay Judas for betraying Jesus. When Judas repented and brought again those thirty pieces of silver saying, 'I have sinned in that I have betrayed the innocent blood', they replied, 'What is that to us? see thou to that'. They just 'burned him' and Judas went out and hanged himself.

There are those who have professed to be saved, and, perhaps genuinely, thought they were saved, who eventually discovered that they were never truly saved. To say that such an one is cast forth under the government of God would be a hard thing; there is always hope for such a person. Here it is the wilful assuming of such a position, as Judas did.

In verse 2, there is a branch that is not bearing fruit. This is the carnal Christian, for there is no fruit in his life. In verse 5, there is a branch bringing forth much fruit, which would be the spiritual Christian. However, in verse 6, there is the natural man, 'If a man abide not in me, he is cast forth'.

'If ye abide in me, and my words abide in you, ye shall ask what ye will, and it shall be done unto you', v. 7

In verses 7 and 8, there are three blessed results of abiding in Him and reproducing Christ. The first is that prayer is answered or fulfilled, v. 7. If our prayers are seldom being answered, the reason could be that we are not abiding in Him and His sayings are not abiding in us, for where those things are true 'ye shall ask what ye will, and it shall be done unto you'. Where our hearts are constantly and practically dependent upon Christ and attracted to Him, His words will abide in us. They will form our thoughts and our petitions and what we say will be an echo of what Christ would have said. If we are abiding in Him and His words are abiding in us our prayers will be fulfilled. This is not just knowing the text of the word so that we can teach and preach but it is His sayings having an abiding place in our hearts. They reside there and are cherished. If we abide in Him, and His words abide in us, we will not ask anything that is outside His will. We can then say, as He did, 'I knew that thou hearest me', John 11. 42. It is very much akin to asking in His name which, given His place before the Father, is asking as His representative.

Thus, there are conditions to be fulfilled but answered prayer is the first blessed result of abiding in Him.

'Herein is my Father glorified, that ye bear much fruit; so shall ye be my disciples', v. 8

The second result of abiding in Him is that the Father is glorified by our bearing much fruit. When the Son was here on the earth the Father looked down upon Him continually, and the Father was glorified in the Son. The Son has now gone back to heaven but we are here and, if the Son is here reproduced in us, the Father, who still looks down, will be glorified. These are matters of great importance. We should not merely be content that our sins are forgiven, that we are saved from hell and on our way to heaven; we ought to have concern that the Father will be glorified in our lives as He sees in us a reproduction of His own Son.

The third result of abiding in Him is that we shall be His disciples. This means that we become real witnesses for Christ. The force of the tense here is, 'Ye will have become my disciples', or, better still, 'Ye will have become disciples of mine', meaning 'Ye will have become my disciples indeed'.

The disciples' responsibility to each other, vv. 9-17

It is evident that in this section our Lord is addressing his disciples as the nucleus of the assembly in our day, where His love and His joy are to be shared. How delightful it is to think of the assembly from this standpoint.

Here, the Lord outlines the characteristics of this new company. They abide in Christ's love, vv. 9, 10, and Christ's joy abides in them, v. 11. They are characterized by love one for another, vv. 12, 13; not only are they loved but they are themselves a loving company. They are also a company who enjoy intimacy with Christ as His friends, to whom the secrets of the Father's heart are disclosed, vv. 14, 15. He then speaks of them as a chosen company and a praying company, v. 16, who ask in the enjoyment of the nearness and love and friendship that is theirs.

'As the Father hath loved me, so have I loved you: continue ye in my love', v. 9

In this verse there is an exhortation, whereas in verse 10 there is a promise. The exhortation, 'continue ye in my love', is to continue in His love; the promise is, 'ye shall abide in my love'. Then, in verse 12, the disciples love one another. In a very real and wonderful way we are introduced to the circle of divine love. The Father loves the Son, the Son loves His own, and His own love each other. This is a truth for the enjoyment of our hearts.

The thought in abiding in Christ's love is of simply abiding in a conscious sense of the enjoyment of Christ's love towards us. This is

96

what the Lord desires for us. In verse 10, he sets before us His own example, as He abode in the Father's love by keeping the Father's commandments. Similarly, we abide in His love by keeping His commandments. There are, then, conditions for the enjoyment of Christ's love. The pleasure the Father had in the Son was because of His obedience to the Father's commandments. It is true that we cannot enter fully into the love of divine persons for each other but what is predominant here in the mind of the Lord is that when He was here He kept His Father's commandments, always abiding in the sense of the Father's love. It is from that standpoint (that love is enjoyed by obedience) that love is brought before us.

Our keeping His commandments does not make Christ love us. He never ceases to love us but if we keep His commandments we are kept in the enjoyment of His love. In contrast, disobedience withdraws us from an enjoyment of that love. Just as there was never a time when the Son was not loved by the Father, so there is never a time when we are not loved by the Son. The Son, as a servant Son, continued in the enjoyment of the Father's love because of His obedience to the Father's commandments. It is the same for us; we continue in the enjoyment of the love of Christ to us as we obey His commandments.

Jude, in verse 21, says, 'Keep yourselves in the love of God'. Again, there is no thought of God ever ceasing to love us, but we are to keep ourselves in the enjoyment of divine love.

Each one is loved but each one does not enjoy that love. John speaks of himself as 'the disciple whom Jesus loved'. This is in chapter 13, where it is said that Jesus 'loved his own'. John is not, therefore, suggesting that Jesus loved him more than the others but is just stating that he was one who was in the enjoyment of His love.

'If ye keep my commandments, ye shall abide in my love; even as I have kept my Father's commandments, and abide in his love', v. 10

In chapter 14 verse 15, He said, 'If ye love me, keep my commandments', but here it is rather different. He says, 'If ye keep my commandments, ye shall abide in my love'. The difference is that in chapter 14 verse 15 keeping His commandments proves our love to Him but here keeping his commandments keeps us in the enjoyment of His love to us. That is how important it is that we should be obedient.

His commandments are not grievous. The commandments contained in the old covenant were grievous, being a burden that they could not bear. The Lord's commandments are not grievous or onerous, however, because we have the power to fulfil them by the indwelling Spirit of God.

In chapter 14 verse 21, there is the present reward for keeping His commandments, which is the enjoyment of the love of the Father and of the Son. Ultimately, our love of the Father and the Son brings enlightenment as to the truth and the wonder of His person, as He will manifest Himself unto us.

'These things have I spoken unto you, that my joy might remain in you, and that your joy might be full', v. 11

The difference between His joy and His love is that we abide in His love whereas His joy abides in us.

'Might remain' is 'might abide', the same word being employed.

It is interesting to observe the two statements 'my joy' and 'your joy'. It is wonderful to think that the Son of God desires that His joy should become our joy. When He speaks of 'my joy' He is not thinking of His joy over them but His own peculiar joy that He experienced while He was here. It was His joy in the Father, the joy of unbroken communion and an unclouded sky.

In Hebrews chapter 12 verse 2, 'the joy that was set before him' is not restricted to the joy of the Father's throne. Rather, it was the joy of doing the Father's will. This enabled Him always to endure the cross and despise the shame. This was beautifully exemplified by our Lord when He was here. For instance, in Matthew chapter 11 verse 26, when those cities in which He performed so many of his mighty miracles rejected Him and He began to upbraid them because they repented not, He says, 'Even so, Father: for so it seemed good in thy sight'. He accepted their rejection because it was good in the sight of His Father. As we gather at the Lord's Supper, we give thanks for the bread and for the cup. We have every reason to do that because of all that means to us, but let us never forget that, when He instituted the supper, He took the bread and the cup and gave thanks for each. No one knew better than He did what these meant and yet He thanked the Father for them because it would mean the accomplishment of the Father's will.

He says these things 'that my joy might remain in you' or 'might abide in you'. He acquainted them with His peculiar joy through what He had told them about it so that it might also become their joy, and that it should become full.

'This is my commandment, That ye love one another, as I have loved you', v. 12

Not only are we loved but we ought to be loving. In verse 12, there is the example of this, and in verse 13 its extent.

It is remarkable that the Lord has to command us to love one another. We ought to love one another without commandment but, of course, there is nothing superfluous in the word of God. It is because of the flesh within us, which may make us envious or suspicious of another, that a commandment is rendered necessary. We do well to search our hearts in this regard. If we do not love each other we fail to keep the command and are disobedient to a divine edict.

The example which they must follow is seen in the expression, 'as I have loved you'. His love included Simon Peter who was going to deny Him and to whom He had to say, in Matthew chapter 16 verse 23, 'Get thee behind me, Satan'. It also included the two sons of thunder to whom He had to say, 'Ye know not what manner of spirit ye are of', Luke 9. 55. It also included Philip, to whom He said in chapter 14 verse 9, 'Have I been so long time with you, and yet hast thou not known me, Philip?' He loved them all with an unselfish love.

The husband's love towards his wife is a rather different love from this. Here we are thinking of love within the sphere of God's family but, although the husband's love to his wife belongs to a different sphere and is of a different character, it is interesting to observe that the example in Ephesians chapter 5 verse 25 is that of Christ's love to the church. The example there is that Christ loved the church and gave Himself for it, in the past, that He might sanctify and cleanse it with the washing of water by the word, in the present, and that He might present it to himself a glorious church, in the future. Paul is indicating there that the love of Christ to the church is the same in the past as it is in the present and as it will be in the future. It never fluctuates and the husband is to love his wife in that way. The love exhibited in courting days, when there was nothing too great to do for her and no sacrifice too much to make for her, is ever to be present.

'Greater love hath no man than this, that a man lay down his life for his friends', v. 13

Here is the extent of our love towards our brethren. We must be prepared to lay down our lives for them. In 1 John chapter 3 verses 16 and 17, John indicates that anyone who says that he is prepared to lay down his life for his brother will not do so if he is not prepared to sacrifice to meet a present need. These things are very practical.

'Ye are my friends, if ye do whatsoever I command you', v. 14

The enjoyment of intimacy is because we are His friends. This is an intimacy greater than that which was enjoyed by Abraham, the friend of God. The principle is the same, that we do not keep things undisclosed from our friends, but the extent of the intimacy here is something that Abraham never touched. He never knew this sphere of divine love, knowing the Father and the Son as we know them.

We saw earlier that there are conditions for the enjoyment of His love. There are terms, too, for the enjoyment of His friendship. The condition for the enjoyment of both His love and His friendship is obedience. He never withdraws his friendship, but our disobedience withdraws us from the enjoyment of it. If we turn to the word of God and do not get help because things are not disclosed to us, it may be because we are not in the good of the fact that intimacies and friendship are enjoyed by those who are obedient.

'Henceforth I call you not servants; for the servant knoweth not what his lord doeth: but I have called you friends; for all things that I have heard of my Father I have made known unto you', v. 15

In the Pauline Epistles, we are described as being slaves, Paul speaking of himself as a bondservant of Jesus Christ. Here, however, the Lord says that He now does not call them slaves but friends. This is not a contradiction. It is a contrast between the relationship in which the disciples once stood and the relationship in which they now stood. Under the law, they were slaves, but now, in the family, they are friends. What characterized them under the law was 'thou shalt' and 'thou shalt not'. The law demanded blind obedience, but this never characterizes friendship. Here, then, the contrast is between law and grace; under the law they were slaves, with blind obedience, but under grace they are friends to whom the secrets and intimacies of the heart are being disclosed. We are not just given duties to perform but, as His friends, the Father's will is opened up to us.

A friend is one who enjoys intimacy. A master never discloses the secrets of his heart to a slave but says 'do this' and 'do that'. Friends, on the other hand, have disclosed to them the intimacies and secrets of another's heart.

'Ye have not chosen me, but I have chosen you, and ordained you, that ye should go and bring forth fruit, and that your fruit should remain: that whatsoever ye shall ask of the Father in my name, he may give it you', v. 16

They were a chosen company. The Lord is not dealing here with being chosen to eternal life, as He is in verse 19, but of being chosen to bring forth fruit. It is friends who are chosen, and they are chosen that they may bring forth quality fruit that abides.

Fruit is not really to do with service but with character. This, then, goes beyond service. It is because He says, 'that ye should go and bring forth fruit' that some might think that this is a mission or a commission, but the word does not mean that. The significance is that He was leaving them and they would be separated from Him, but He had chosen them and ordained them that they should bring forth fruit. His desire for them was to go and reproduce Him against the background of His leaving them.

For asking 'in my name' refer to chapter 14 verse 13 and chapter 16 verse 23.

'These things I command you, that ye love one another', v. 17

In this verse, the Lord Jesus says to His disciples, 'These things I command you, that ye love one another' but, in verse 18, they find themselves in the outside world. Up to this point, the Lord has been directing our attention to that inner circle of the disciples, which was the nucleus of the assembly, where Christ's joy is shared and His love is enjoyed, but, in verse 18, we move out to the world where we experience its hate and where, by the gracious help of the Spirit of God, we bear testimony to Christ.

The disciples' responsibility towards the world, vv. 18-27

In verses 18 to 27, His own are seen as His witnesses. In this section, which continues to chapter 16 verse 4, we are directed to the fact that we have been left in the world so that through the Holy Spirit we might be a testimony to it. There are, then, two worlds. There is the world of love and joy and the world of hatred and persecution. A great tragedy is that so many Christians are today trying to make the best of both worlds, something that we can never do if we belong to Christ. We have to make our choice. We are either going to enjoy the intimacy of Christ's friendship, His joy and love being very real to us, with the consequent hatred of the world or else we are going to settle down in this world, experiencing little of its hatred and persecution and never enjoying the intimacies of the Father's heart, the joy of Christ, and all that it means to abide in His love.

In verse 26, the Lord Jesus says, 'But when the Comforter is come, whom I will send unto you from the Father, even the Spirit of truth, which proceedeth from the Father, he shall testify of me'. This is the section which deals in particular with the Holy Spirit and the fact that both He and we are in the world to bear testimony to Christ. It is interesting in this section, as we read of our responsibility to be a testimony to the world, that the Lord Jesus unfolds to us its true character. This is something necessary to understand. In verse 19, He speaks of the world's love, but in verse 25 He speaks of its hatred. The world loves its own, but in verse 25 the Lord says, 'They hated me without a cause'. The reason for this world's hatred is twofold. It is because the child of God is not of the world, v. 19, and the world does not know God, v. 21. We find ourselves in a world to which we do not belong, out of which we have been chosen, and, because we are not of the world, we can only expect its hatred. We also find ourselves in a world that does not know God and because of this we can expect to be hated and persecuted.

In verses 22 and 24, the Lord Jesus makes it clear that there is no excuse for this world's hatred. Twice over we have the expression 'they had not had sin'. God's Son had been here and because they had heard the testimony of His words and seen the testimony of His works the world was without excuse; otherwise, 'they had not had sin'. The divine conclusion concerning the world after that Christ has been in it is found in verse 24, 'but now have they both seen and hated both me and my Father'. What a significant statement! The words that He spoke and the works that He performed were all given to Him by the Father and in them there was a complete revelation of the Father's heart. When they hated the Son, they also hated the Father. In addition, when the Son went back to heaven, He sent down the Holy Spirit, who has proceeded from the Father, that the Spirit might bear witness to the one whom the world has hated.

'If the world hate you, ye know that it hated me before it hated you', v. 18

'If the world hate you', it does so because it hates the Father and the Son. We are just experiencing what God's Son Himself experienced when He was here.

'If ye were of the world, the world would love his own: but because ye are not of the world, but I have chosen you out of the world, therefore the world hateth you', v. 19

In chapter 13 verse 1, we read that, 'having loved his own which were in the world, he loved them unto the end'. How glad we may be that this is the company amongst whom we are numbered, His own who are loved by Him. In this verse there is another company, the world's own, who are loved by the world. The world loves his own but the love that we enjoy is the love of God's Son, the love of the Father and love amongst ourselves.

The world's love is selfish and its hatred, v. 25, is unrighteous.

The Greek word *kosmos*, 'the world', is used in the scriptures in a variety of settings. Sometimes it is used for the material universe but it is also used for the world of humanity, as in John chapter 1 verse 10, which says, 'He was in the world, and the world was made by him, and the world knew him not'. He was in the material world and the world of humanity knew Him not. The word is also used in a moral sense, describing that world system that embraces different races, classes of people and religions. It is estranged from God, is happy to live apart from Him and hates Him. This is the sense of 'the world' in this verse. It is never expected that the Christian should conform to the world, because he has been individually chosen out of it.

The Lord says, 'ye are not of the world'. The fact that we are not of the world brings upon us the world's hatred. The other reason for the world's hatred, v. 21, is that the world does not know God. 'Hateful and hating one another' is the way the unregenerate are described in Titus chapter 3 verse 3. This is the character of the world.

The fact that 'I have chosen you out of the world' is beyond our understanding. It relates to the solemn and divine call in the gospel. In verse 16, they were chosen to bring forth fruit, but here is the sovereign choice of God in the gospel. This makes nothing of us but everything of Him. There is nothing so humbling as to think that we have been chosen out of the world and, because of this, it is not our lot to complain about the fact the world hates us. We are not hated so much because we are chosen but because we are not of the world. That choice has taken us out of the world, so we live in it as those who are not of it.

The reason why so many of us do not experience the hatred and persecution of the world is because we are far too like the world, not living true to the fact of having been chosen out of it. We are glad we are not of this world as far as its condemnation is concerned, that we are not hastening to hell and the lake of fire, but let us be true, day by day, to the fact that we 'are not of the world'. Its pursuits and pleasures are different to ours and it is because of this the world hates us.

'Remember the word that I said unto you, The servant is not greater than his lord. If they have persecuted me, they will also persecute you; if they have kept my saying, they will keep yours also', v. 20

Undoubtedly, He is referring here to chapter 13 verse 16 in connection with feet-washing, where He said, 'The servant is not greater than His lord'. The teaching there is that, if we refuse or fail to follow His example and wash the saints' feet, we are setting ourselves up as being greater than our Lord. The Lord is there impressing the disciples with their responsibility, as teachers, to do as He did. Here, He is teaching that we cannot expect better treatment than He received. He was hated and so will we be hated. The character of this world's hatred is that it is prepared to go to the length of persecution.

Then, He says, 'If they have kept my saying, they will keep yours also'. Oftentimes we find it very disappointing when the world rejects what we have to say, but the Saviour says they did the same to Him.

'But all these things will they do unto you for my name's sake, because they know not him that sent me', v. 21

It is not that they do not know that God sent the Son, but they do not know the God who sent Him. This is why the world persecutes us.

'For my name's sake' indicates that it is because of our identification with the person of Christ, His work, His glory and all that is involved in His name, that we are persecuted. The disciples were very soon to experience this, realizing how true these words of the Saviour were. In John chapter 20 verse 19, 'the doors were shut . . . for fear of the Jews'. In Acts chapter 5, able-bodied apostles were beaten in an attempt to intimidate them, but they left the council 'rejoicing that they were counted worthy to suffer shame for his name', v. 41. This continues throughout the book of Acts. They remembered, no doubt, the words of the Lord to His Father in John chapter 17 verse 25, 'O righteous Father, the world hath not known thee'.

The difference between us and the world around us is that we know God but the world does not know Him. It is for this reason that we are persecuted.

Chapter 16 verse 1 makes it clear that He was telling them these things to sustain them in persecution, so that they should not stumble.

'If I had not come and spoken unto them, they had not had sin: but now they have no cloke for their sin', v. 22

They had no excuse for their hatred. Here, they have no cloke for their sin because of the words that He spoke. In chapter 7 verses 45 and 46, the chief priests and the Pharisees sent officers to arrest Him and when they came back without Him the chief priests and officers questioned them, 'Why have ye not brought him? The officers answered, 'Never man spake like this man'. There we see the testimony of His words. Then, in verse 24, there is the testimony of His works. 'If I had not done among them the works which none other man did, they had not had sin'. In chapter 11 verse 47, after the raising of Lazarus, when the Jews believed on Him, the chief priests and the Pharisees said, 'What do we?

106

for this man doeth many miracles'. They could not resist the works that He did and, therefore, because of the testimony of His words and works they were left without excuse. They had no cloak, pretext or pretence for their sin.

He referred repeatedly to the fact that not only was He sent but that He came, involving His deity. He was 'sent' as a servant; He 'came' in relation to the fact of His deity. He came voluntarily from a pre-existent state. In chapter 18 verse 37, Pilate asked Him the question, 'Art Thou a king?' Jesus answered, 'Thou sayest that I am a king. To this end was I born, and for this cause came I into the world, that I should bear witness unto the truth'. Our Saviour was 'born', reminding us of His true manhood, and He 'came', indicating His deity.

'He that hateth me hateth my Father also. If I had not done among them the works which none other man did, they had not had sin: but now have they both seen and hated both me and my Father', vv. 23, 24

Here is the conclusion: 'but now they have both seen and hated both me and my Father'. As has already been observed, the Father's heart had been revealed, not only in Christ's words but in His works, and the world that saw and hated the Son saw and hated the Father.

'But this cometh to pass, that the word might be fulfilled that is written in their law, They hated me without a cause', v. 25

The world's hatred is an unrighteous hatred, for it hates without a cause. This is a quotation from Psalm 69, prophetically spoken in respect of the Lord Jesus Christ. Some might say that the Psalms are not the law, but we need to observe that the word 'law' is used in a threefold way in the New Testament. Sometimes it refers only to the decalogue, the ten commandments. At other times, it refers only to the Pentateuch, the first five books of the Bible. However, in John chapter 12 verse 34, the word 'law' is used in respect of the whole Old Testament, as it is here.

There would be no need for directions of this nature if there were no danger involved. John says, in 1 John chapter 2 verses 15 and 16, 'Love not the world, neither the things that are in the world. If any man love the world, the love of the Father is not in him. For all that is in the world, the lust of the flesh, and the lust of the eyes, and the pride of life, is not of the Father, but is of the world'. This is an exposure of what is contained in this world system estranged from God.

In Romans chapter 3 verse 24, the Apostle Paul speaks of the fact that we are 'justified freely by his grace through the redemption that is in Christ Jesus'. The word 'freely' is the same as that which is here translated 'without a cause'. It is the same word as Paul uses in 2 Corinthians chapter 11 verse 7, where he says, 'I have preached to you the gospel of God freely'. Thus, we were justified gratuitously, without a cause, for nothing, because we were sinners without merit, bankrupt and without means. God moved towards us and has justified us by His grace.

'But when the Comforter is come, whom I will send unto you from the Father, even the Spirit of truth, which proceedeth from the Father, he shall testify of me', v. 26

Three words are used here in relation to the Comforter: He comes, He is sent and He proceeds from the Father.

'But when the Comforter is come' emphasizes His deity. Christ came and the Spirit came and in this there is reference to the deity both of Christ and the Spirit. 'Whom I will send' indicates that He not only came but He was sent on a mission. The word used, *pempō*, is not an official sending so much as it is the fact of sending, the sender becoming an escort. The one who was sent is accompanied by the sender and so the Lord sends Him and accompanies Him. A great deal has been said on 'which proceedeth from the Father'. In view of the fact that it is in the present continuous tense some speak in terms of an eternal procession of the Spirit from the Father. That is a bit illogical and He is, in fact, just speaking of the character of the Spirit. Proceeding is different from coming and being sent and has in view the object for which the person is sent. Accordingly, the fact that He 'comes' relates to His deity, His

108

being sent relates to His mission and 'proceedeth' relates to the object for which He is sent.

This is borne out by the occurrences of the verb 'proceed' in the scriptures. It is the word that the Lord uses in Matthew chapter 4 verse 4, 'Man shall not live by bread alone, but by every word that proceedeth out of the mouth of God'. Every word that proceedeth out of the mouth of God has its effect on the life of the individual. Again, in Mark chapter 7 verses 21 and 22, the Lord Jesus said, 'For from within, out of the heart of men, proceed evil thoughts, adulteries, fornications, murders, thefts, covetousness, wickedness, deceit, lasciviousness, an evil eye, blasphemy, pride, foolishness'. It begins in the heart and then there is the effect, the awful deed. It is a poor illustration of what we have here but it gives us the idea. The word 'proceedeth' is not just His being sent but it has to do with the fulfilment of the purpose for which He is sent. The coming of the Comforter is associated with both the Father and the Son. The simple reason for this is that the world hated Christ and, in doing so, also hated the Father. When the world despised the works and the words of Christ, they despised the works and words that the Father gave to Christ. The Son was the full revelation of the Father so that to hate the one was to hate the other. Not only did the world hate the Son of God but it gave Him a cross and sent Him out of this world. People lose interest in those who hate them, but this is not so with divine persons. The Father and the Son were hated by the world but, when the Son went back to heaven, He sent the Spirit from the Father in order that the Spirit might continue to bear testimony to that world.

The Holy Spirit testified through the disciples. In Acts chapter 5 verse 32, Peter said, 'we are his witnesses of these things; and so is also the Holy Ghost, whom God hath given to them that obey him'. The apostles saw Christ and all that happened to Him and became witnesses, but the Holy Spirit witnesses through us, who have not seen Him.

The Holy Spirit was testifying through Stephen. Acts chapter 7 verses 55 and 56 says, 'he, being full of the Holy Ghost, looked up stedfastly into heaven, and saw the glory of God, and Jesus standing on the right hand of God, and said, Behold, I see the heavens opened, and the Son of man standing on the right hand of God'. And it is interesting to observe

109

that the testimony of Stephen was the testimony almost akin to that of Jesus when He was here. On the cross, Jesus said, 'Father, forgive them; for they know not what they do', Luke 23. 34. Stephen, through the Holy Spirit, said, 'Lord, lay not this sin to their charge', Acts 7. 60. On the cross, Jesus said, 'Father, into thy hands I commend my spirit', Luke 23. 46. Stephen, full of the Holy Spirit, said, 'Lord Jesus, receive my spirit', Acts 7. 59. What a testimony this was, a man through the Holy Spirit perpetuating what had been seen in Jesus when He was here.

'And ye also shall bear witness, because ye have been with me from the beginning', v. 27

Invariably the expression 'from the beginning' in Luke chapter 1 verse 2, here and 1 John chapter 1 verse 1, has to do with the beginning of our Lord's public ministry. He is speaking to men who were with Him from the beginning of His public ministry and who would bear witness because of this. The Holy Spirit would also bear witness through them. There is an important principle here. The secret of effective witness is living with Christ, 'because ye have been with me'. We are here as His witnesses, chosen out of the world and sent back into it to be witnesses. Living in the world but not of it, hated by it, the object of its persecution but effective witnesses as we live with Him.

There is a great cry today that unless we compromise with the men and women of the world and the young people of the world, we will never win them for Christ. It is said, that we should frequent the places that they frequent, dress the way they dress, conforming to the fashions of the world around us, and that if they see us so different to them we will never reach them or win them. Nothing is further from the mind of God in the matter of witness than that. He says, 'I have chosen you out of the world'. They were not of the world and would be hated and persecuted by it. The secret of effective witness is to learn to live with Him. When the world looks on us, they should not find in us those whose lives console them but those whose lives condemn them, being altogether different from theirs.

Chapter 16

The Lord continues speaking of His Spirit in the world and in the believer. He also continues to speak here of His going away, in respect of which He uses different words. In verse 5, where He says, 'But now I go my way to Him that sent me', the word simply means 'a withdrawal': 'I withdraw to him that sent Me'. In verse 7, where He says, 'It is expedient for you that I go away', the word involves a separation. Also, in verse 7, 'if I depart', and verse 28, 'I leave the world, and go to the Father', it is not just withdrawal or separation, but an end is in view. The Lord is undoubtedly seeking to prepare, enlighten and encourage the disciples for the great change that would take place after He left. He refers repeatedly to the time that shall come, in verses 2, 4, 25, and 32.

There is a broad twofold division in this chapter. From verses 1 to 16, He speaks of His going away from the standpoint of the coming of the Comforter, but in verses 17 to 33 He speaks of His going away from the standpoint of His being with the Father. His going away would, therefore, involve two things. First, it would involve the coming of the Comforter. In verse 7, He says, 'It is expedient for you that I go away: for if I go not away, the Comforter will not come unto you'. In verse 13, He says, 'When he, the Spirit of truth, is come'. The character of the present day is that our Lord is absent, but the Comforter is present. Second, His going away would involve His being with the Father and so, in verse 17, He says, 'Because I go to the Father', in verse 25, 'I shall shew you plainly of the Father' and in verse 28, 'I leave the world, and go to the Father'.

The Comforter down here would look after their interests on earth and the Son would look after their interests in heaven, representing the interests before the Father.

The Lord's going away and the coming of the Comforter, vv. 1-16

'These things have I spoken unto you, that ye should not be offended', v. 1

In verses 1 to 4, future comfort is assured to the disciples by reason of the Lord's full knowledge. In verse 4, He says, 'these things have I told you, that when the time shall come, ye may remember that I told you of them'. He is telling them that when these things overtake them they could be comforted by the fact that He knew about them and had told them about them. He was prepared to support them in these circumstances that were known to Him, and what was true for the disciples is true for us. We can be assured that nothing overtakes us that He did not know about in advance and, in every circumstance, He can help and support us.

In chapter 13, the Lord Jesus tells them of their coming persecution and the hatred they would experience. He tells them that He Himself had already experienced this and then, in chapter 16, He further develops this. In the opening verses, He discloses to them the nature of this persecution so that they might not be stumbled. This has to be understood in the light of these disciples being converted Jews. Persecution and martyrdom would come at the hands of their own fellow Jews who would think that they were doing God service.

'These things' might refer to the ministry in a general way but would undoubtedly refer to chapter 15 verses 18 to 27, where He has spoken to them of this world's persecution and hatred.

'That ye should not be offended' means 'that ye should not be stumbled'. The thought of stumbling is of stumbling over an obstacle. The great obstacle to the converted Jew would be persecution from his own people against the background of their own national aspirations and hopes.

'They shall put you out of the synagogues: yea, the time cometh, that whosoever killeth you will think that he doeth God service', v. 2

The persecution would be twofold in its nature, involving excommunication and martyrdom. They would deem them not fit for Jewish privileges and put them out of their synagogues; and they would also now deem them not fit to live and would kill them. To be put out of the synagogue meant the loss of fellowship, family and social privileges. This persecution from sincere religious motives still happens today. Religious people, who are most sincere in their ignorance, are often more ruthless in their persecution than those who make no confession at all. The Lord discovered that when He was here, and His people know this as well.

When they excommunicated them, they would profess that they had divine authority over this, and they would protest that they were doing God service. They were zealous of divine interests and sincerely ignorant in their excommunication of those converted Jews.

The tense here is not 'killeth' but 'killed'. They could not kill without authority but they would go to the extent of obtaining this and kill, thinking they were offering service to God. This is the same word as in Hebrews chapter 9 verse 1, 'ordinances of divine service'. This was not, therefore, just the thought that they were doing a good work, but they did it professing utter devotion to God. Of course, in Romans chapters 10 and 11, we learn that blindness and hardness has overtaken the nation until the fulness of the Gentiles be come in. This is judicial hardening because of the crucifixion of the Messiah.

What the Lord Jesus warns about did happen. What comfort it must have been for them to know that this had not taken the Lord by surprise. He knew all about it and therefore He could support them in it.

'And these things will they do unto you, because they have not known the Father, nor me', v. 3

The emphasis is upon the actions rather than the objects. In 'because they have not known the Father, nor me' the word for 'known', *ginōskō*, signifies that they have not 'recognized'. It is important to note that it is not just ignorance, because they had the opportunity to recognize but refused to do so. Their ignorance is wilful.

'But these things have I told you, that when the time shall come, ye may remember that I told you of them. And these things I said not unto you at the beginning, because I was with you', v. 4

'The time' is 'the hour'. The Lord is indicating, for their assurance, that He knew all about this hour, which was now appointed for these things. Because these trials were known to Christ, He could succour them and, if need be, deliver them.

'These things', about which He has been speaking, belong to the time of His absence. When He was with them and was the special object of the attack, He protected them. When He was questioned about His disciples and His doctrine, He just spoke about His doctrine, saying nothing about His disciples. In chapter 18 verse 8, He says, 'if therefore ye seek me, let these go their way'.

'At the beginning' is 'from the beginning'. It is the same expression as in chapter 6 verse 64, 'Jesus knew from the beginning who they were that believed not, and who should betray him' and in chapter 15 verse 27, 'ye have been with me from the beginning'. They had already known persecution but what they were to experience afterwards would be for a different reason. In Matthew chapter 10 verses 16 to 18, He had warned them, 'Behold, I send you forth as sheep in the midst of wolves: be ye therefore wise as serpents, and harmless as doves. But beware of men: for they will deliver you up to the councils, and they will scourge you in their synagogues; and ye shall be brought before governors and kings for my sake, for a testimony against them and the Gentiles'. He was warning them there as a Jewish remnant, but what He is warning them of here is what would befall them as Christians, particularly in the time of His absence. Historians tell us that all the apostles, without exception, suffered martyrdom.

He said to them in chapter 13 verse 19, 'I tell you before it come, that, when it is come to pass, ye may believe that I am'. They would know His deity, that He foreknew because He was God. Here, however, it is not they would know His deity but that here was one who knew what was going to come to pass. In this He could comfort them and, if need be, He would deliver them.

'But now I go my way to him that sent me; and none of you asketh me, Whither goest thou?' v. 5

In verses 5 to 7, He speaks of their future profit by reason of the coming of the Comforter. He was going to leave them, but the Comforter would come.

The word that the Lord employs in 'I go', *hupagō*, means 'I withdraw', yet none of them demanded, 'Whither goest thou?' In chapter 13 verse 36, Peter had said, 'Lord, whither goest thou?' and, in chapter 14 verse 5, Thomas had said, 'Lord, we know not whither thou goest'. Both Peter and Thomas, therefore, had asked this very question and yet the Lord Jesus now says, 'none of you asketh me, Whither goest Thou?' When they had asked Him that question, He had read their hearts and knew the motive which prompted them to ask. They knew what His departure would mean to them in respect of the sorrow that they would experience, but they had not asked the question, 'Lord whither goest thou?' in terms of what it would mean to Him and what particular profit it would bring to them. He now deals with this. He was going back as the sent one, in virtue of an assignment fulfilled, a mission completed and a work finished, and this would bring undoubted profit for them and joy to Him.

They had not understood the Son as the revealer of the Father, or that the Father had given Him not just the throne of David or an earthly kingdom but had given Him all things. He points out later that, as yet, they were not able to bear these things; they did not yet have the capacity to understand and appreciate them.

In chapter 14 verse 5, they knew the way but they were not quite assured of 'whither'. They were thinking in terms of the Father's house at Jerusalem, something earthly. The Lord goes on to tell them that, predominantly, it was not a better place to which He was going but to the Father. They knew the way, but they did not know the fact that He was going to a person. In Luke chapter 24 verse 26, it is clear that from the prophets they should have known that the Messiah would suffer and 'enter into his glory'. 'Glory' is, in fact, plural, the reference being to His present and future glories. However, after all the prophets had said, they did not understand. Of course, we have to understand these things against their Jewish expectations of an earthly Messiah setting up an earthly kingdom.

Their incredulity in respect of His rising again was made all the worse in that the chief priests and Pharisees knew what He had said about it, but the disciples had forgotten. They were blinded by reason of the fact that they believed in a delivering Messiah who would set up His kingdom, whereas the chief priests and Pharisees had not been looking for Him to set up a kingdom, imagining that He was an impostor. That is why, in 1 Corinthians chapter 1 verse 23, it states, 'we preach Christ crucified, unto the Jews a stumblingblock, and unto the Greeks foolishness'. The Jews generally can only think of an all-conquering, victorious Messiah, not of the Messiah going to a cross.

'But because I have said these things unto you, sorrow hath filled your heart', v. 6

'These things' relates to their excommunication and martyrdom and, for this reason, they are sorrowful. There is even more sorrow within the disciples that day. They had thought that His mission as the Messiah was now a complete failure, despite the fact that He had promised that He would come to them, and for them, and that He would manifest Himself to them, thus never leaving them as orphans. They had been asking further details with regard to His glorification and their blessing, and their hearts just filled with sorrow and despondency.

'Nevertheless I tell you the truth; It is expedient for you that I go away: for if I go not away, the Comforter will not come unto you; but if I depart, I will send him unto you', v. 7

'I tell you the truth' is not just an indication that He would not tell them a lie, but a statement that He was telling what is, in fact, the truth. There was error in their mind with regard to what was going to happen, and He wanted now to tell them the truth. The error in their mind, which arose because of their Jewish expectation, was with regard to the significance of His departure.

The truth was that 'It is expedient for you that I go away'. 'Expedient' is the same word, *sumpherō*, as is used by Caiaphas in chapter 11 verse 50 and chapter 18 verse 14. The word has deeper significance than 'it is necessary', signifying 'it is profitable'. Profit was going to come to the disciples by reason of the Lord going away from them. It is the same word as in 1 Corinthians chapter 6 verse 12, 'All things are lawful unto me, but all things are not expedient', or 'not profitable'.

When Jesus was here the Holy Spirit abode upon Him, John 1. 32, sealed Him, 6. 27, and anointed Him, Luke 4. 18. The Holy Spirit could do this because Jesus was sinless. However, the Holy Spirit could only indwell us on the ground of redemption accomplished and Christ exalted. It is because redemption has been accomplished and Christ exalted that the Holy Spirit has now been sent to indwell and to work in the believer as He has never worked before in any man or woman. By reason of the indwelling of the Spirit they would be linked with Christ in glory and this would eclipse knowing Him as the Messiah. Their Jewish expectation was to be associated with Messiah reigning on the earth, but the Lord tells them that there is something more profitable to them than that. He would go, the Comforter would come, and they would be linked with Him where He is in the presence of His Father.

There is further profit. When He was here, He said, 'I am . . . the truth' but now the Comforter would come, who is 'the Spirit of truth' and He would 'guide them into all truth'. Also, we noticed in John chapter 14 verse 16 that He said He would send another Comforter, not another 'instead of' but another 'in addition to'. There was profit, therefore, in

117

that they would have an additional Comforter. The Lord Jesus would remain the Comforter on the throne and they would have another Comforter, indwelling them, in addition to Him. There are never two divine persons on earth at the same time; when the Lord was here the Spirit was absent but now the Lord has gone the Spirit is present. 'It is expedient', or 'profitable', has in view, therefore, the contrast between what He was to them when He was here and what He and the Spirit would be to them when He was absent. When He was here, they had recourse to Him in all their difficulties and He gave them understanding of the scriptures. He tells them that the Holy Spirit will do for them what He has been doing for them; He is the Spirit of truth who will also guide them.

In verse 5, it says, 'I go . . . to Him that sent me', in verse 10, 'I go to my Father', but here it is just, 'I go away'. Thus, the Lord implied here that His going away would involve separation from them. 'For if I go not away, the Comforter will not come unto you'. Chapter 7 verse 39 says, 'the Holy Ghost was not yet given; because that Jesus was not yet glorified'. It was necessary that Jesus should go away and be glorified on the Father's throne before the Comforter would come, though here there is not so much the idea of His glorification but His being with the Father and His separation from them.

In chapter 14 verse 17, we observed the language of the Saviour concerning the Comforter, 'the Spirit of truth; whom the world cannot receive'. He would come unto the disciples, but the world cannot receive Him.

Then, He says, 'but if I depart [the thought of departing to a goal], I will send him unto you'. In chapter 15 verse 26, He says of the Comforter, 'whom I will send unto you from the Father'. In that verse the first personal pronoun 'I' is emphatic, emphasizing the sender. Here, however, the emphasis is not on the one who sends but on the mission upon which the Comforter is sent. This is an important distinction.

In the Old Testament, the Holy Spirit indwelt men, such as Bezaleel, only for a special work and not permanently. As John chapter 7 verse 39 says, 'the Holy Ghost was not yet given'. He had never been given in

Old Testament times in the sense of an abiding presence. What you have in connection with the Spirit in chapter 14 verse 16 is that 'he may abide with you forever'. The Lord is saying, 'as long as you are here, He will be here and will never leave you'. Paul says in Ephesians chapter 4 verse 30, 'And grieve not the holy Spirit of God, whereby ye are sealed unto the day of redemption'. Though we might grieve Him, He will still remain with us. We are sealed by Him, something that was never enjoyed in the Old Testament.

The word 'Comforter' does not carry the sense of one who brings solace but of one who would be their counsellor and their advocate. He would minister the joy that would displace their sorrow, although, even before the Spirit was given, they had joy in His resurrection. John chapter 20 verse 20 says, 'Then were the disciples glad, when they saw the Lord'. However, that gladness was just a foretaste of a fuller gladness when the Comforter would come.

'And when he is come, he will reprove the world of sin, and of righteousness, and of judgment', v. 8

In verses 8 to 11, future enlightenment is assured to them by the Holy Spirit as to the character of this present world.

Some think of this as the Spirit convicting the sinner of his need, v. 9; that there is righteousness secured in Christ through His death and resurrection, and that the righteousness of God is now available, v. 10. However, the phrase 'ye see me no more', in verse 10, hardly fits with the idea of the righteousness of God secured in a man at God's right hand.

The rendering of 'when He is come' is really, 'and having come' This word 'come', as we have seen already, is used frequently of the Spirit. Examples of this are found in chapter 15 verse 26, 'when the Comforter is come' and chapter 16 verse 13, 'Howbeit when he, the Spirit of truth, is come'. Here it is not 'is come' but He is anticipating the Spirit having come.

119

Now there are three matters we have to consider in these verses in order to rightly arrive at the significance of the Lord's teaching, the first of which is the significance of the word 'reprove'. The Revised Version says 'convict', the New Translation says, 'bring demonstration'. The word is used in chapter 3 verse 20, 'For every one that doeth evil hateth the light, neither cometh to the light, lest his deeds should be reproved'. Their deeds would be reproved by their coming to the light. It is also used in chapter 8 verse 9, 'And they which heard it, being convicted by their own conscience, went out one by one, beginning at the eldest, even unto the last'. If a person is convicted, then an effect has been produced.

The English word 'convict' can be used in terms of convicting of sin but hardly in terms of convicting of righteousness and of judgement. The word has, rather, the thought of 'bringing a demonstration'. It supposes the action of the Spirit, though what is emphasized here is the presence of the Spirit in a believer rather than His actions. This brings a demonstration to the world of sin, of righteousness and of judgement. This is not the Spirit of God convicting the individual sinner; it is the Spirit of God in the believer. He said in verse 7, 'It is expedient for you that I go away: for if I go not away, the Comforter will not come unto you; but if I depart, I will send him unto you', and having come unto you He will bring demonstration to the world of sin, of righteousness, and of judgement, by reason of His coming unto you. He does not speak of His coming unto the world but 'unto you'.

The Lord is not speaking here of the work of the Comforter with a view to the salvation of the sinner but rather a demonstration to the world of sin, of righteousness and of judgement by reason of the Comforter's presence in, and working through, the believer. Some think that what the Lord was teaching here was that He would convict the world of sin, that man is fallen; He would convict the world of righteousness, that the sinner needs to turn to Christ; He would convict the world of judgement, that judgement that remains for those who are without Christ. Some think this but the Saviour says, 'I will send him unto you'.

Second, there is the subject of the Comforter's reproof, which is 'the world'. As we have just noted it is the Comforter coming 'unto you', and

He will convict not the sinner but the world. He will bring demonstration to the world of these three matters by indwelling and working through the believer.

Third, in verses 9 to 11, there is the substance of His reproof. He shall reprove the world concerning sin, and righteousness, and judgement. The setting of this is that He was rejected, because they would not believe on Him, and He had to go to the Father because there was no righteousness down here. He would send the Spirit as the One who would make demonstration of these important facts.

'Of sin, because they believe not on me', v. 9

He would reprove the world concerning sin, not because they have not kept the law but 'because they believe not on me'. The sin of the world is that God has been fully manifested here in the person of His Son, but men believed Him not. They rejected Him when He was here and the Comforter's presence in the Christian is a demonstration that the world is under sin.

'Of righteousness, because I go to my Father, and ye see me no more', v. 10

The Spirit would also bring demonstration to the world concerning righteousness, because 'I go to my Father'. It is not really 'my Father' but 'the Father'. The Comforter demonstrates not only the presence of sin in the world but also the absence of righteousness. They 'denied the Holy One and the Just', Acts 3. 14, when He was here, and slew Him, and because of this He has had to go back to the Father. The world, as such, will never behold Him in grace again, though it will see Him in judgement.

Thus, not only is the world under sin but righteousness is absent from it, because they have slain the Just One.

The world can only see this as the Spirit of God demonstrates these things through us day by day. The world sees the reality of our

121

profession of faith, the reality of our being a Christian, the reality of our trust in a man who has gone away.

Hebrews chapter 11 verse 7 says, 'By faith Noah, being warned of God of things not seen as yet, moved with fear, prepared an ark to the saving of his house; by the which he condemned the world, and became heir of the righteousness which is by faith'. Noah's act of faith did two things: it saved him; and condemned the world. That is what we have here.

'Of judgment, because the prince of this world is judged', v. 11

The Holy Spirit would also reprove the world concerning judgement, 'because the prince of this world is judged'. This may be rendered, 'the ruler of this world hath been judged'. The idea here is that the world was a tool of Satan, who, from the beginning, had endeavoured to defeat God's purpose. At Calvary, Satan appeared to be victorious, but God raised His Son and glorified Him, and the Comforter is come; in the believer there is a demonstration of the judgement of the world in its ruler. The world is judged in its ruler because the world under that ruler condemned Christ to death.

Judgement is always present, a present sentence passed, whereas condemnation is future, the execution of a sentence. Here it is not condemnation but judgement, the passing of a sentence, because the prince of this world having been judged, the sentence has been passed on him. The sentence has been passed but not yet executed. Until then he goes about as a roaring lion, 1 Pet. 5. 8. The Lord said in John chapter 12 verse 31, 'Now is the judgment of this world: now shall the prince of this world be cast out'. He was anticipating this very thing.

There is a difference between the prince of this world and the prince of the power of the air. The prince of this world is in relation to the subjects upon whom he operates. He operates upon a world that is estranged from God. The word *kosmos* has a threefold significance: it speaks of the material universe; the world of humanity; or a system that is estranged from God and is content to live without Him. However, when Paul speaks of the prince of the power of the air, in Ephesians chapter 2 verse 2, there are three expressions to note, namely the prince, the authority and the air. There it is his rule over the authority of the evil spirits in the air, the domain in which he operates. It is amazing to think that the very air that we breathe is the sphere of the devil's operation and thus his influence, authority and power are pervasive. We can now understand why Paul says, 'be not conformed to this world', Rom. 12. 2. No child of God should want to conform to a world who has the devil for its god.

Every reference to the devil as the prince of this world is before Calvary. Thereafter, he is called its god, 2 Cor. 4. 4. There is a difference. Calvary has constituted the devil the god of this world. Up until then he was its ruler but now he is its god, because under him the world condemned God's Son to death. It was at Calvary that this world's iniquity became full, that its sin was made patent. Thus, at Calvary the world was exposed as now having the devil as its god.

The devil had already tempted Him, and this had proven to the devil that he had nothing in Him. In John chapter 14 verse 30, he makes a fresh attack. 'Hereafter I will not talk much with you: for the prince of this world cometh, and hath nothing in me'. The sense there is that the devil had nothing in Him over which he had power, especially in the sense of the power of death. This serves to demonstrate that our Lord's death was voluntary.

To summarize, the Spirit of God in the believer demonstrates that the world is under sin because it rejected the man who had been with the Father. The Spirit of God in the believer demonstrates to the world that righteousness is absent, because they condemned the only righteous man. The Spirit of God in the believer is a demonstration that the world is hastening for judgement because under its prince it condemned this self-same one. Christianity in the power of the Spirit is a demonstration of these tremendously important truths.

'I have yet many things to say unto you, but ye cannot bear them now', v. 12

If, in verses 8 to 11, there is a demonstration to this present world, in verses 12 to 15 there is enlightenment as to the world to come. Notice, especially, what the Lord says in verse 13.

In these verses, broadly speaking, the Lord is teaching them that the Spirit of truth would continue, in His absence, the ministry that He had Himself commenced. In chapter 14 verse 6, He says, 'I am the truth' and, in chapter 16 verse 13, the Spirit is 'the Spirit of truth'. In chapter 14 verse 6, He says, 'I am the way', and He says of the Comforter, in chapter 16 verse 13, 'He will guide you'. In chapter 5 verse 19, the Son said, 'The Son can do nothing of Himself', meaning that He could not act independently of the Father, and of the Spirit He says, 'he shall not speak of himself', 16. 13. He says in chapter 15 verse 15, 'all things that I have heard of my Father I have made known unto you', and of the Spirit He says, in chapter 16 verse 13, 'whatsoever he shall hear, that shall he speak'. What the Son had been doing when He was with them, the Spirit would continue to do once He was absent. This is further proof of the profit that would be theirs by the coming of the Spirit.

The Lord speaks of the ministry of the Spirit in a twofold way. In respect of the disciples, 'he will guide you', v. 13; in respect of the Lord, 'He shall glorify me', v. 14. He will guide you into all 'the truth' because He will speak whatever He shall hear; He will glorify me, for 'he shall receive of mine'.

'I have yet many things to say unto you' would, no doubt, involve the whole canon of scripture.

'Now', at this time, is the same word that is used in chapter 13 verse 33, 'so now I say to you'. At this particular time, they did not have the spiritual capacity to bear the things He would have said to them because they had not yet received the Spirit. Again, therefore, we can understand the profit they would have by the coming of the Comforter. The Spirit would make known to them, broadly speaking, the 'all things'

124

that the Father would give to the Son, which belong to Him now. They did not have the capacity to receive these things because, first, they were still thinking in terms of an earthly Messiah rather than in terms of the one who would receive all things from the Father, and, second, as yet they did not have the Comforter, the Holy Spirit.

He had told them many things and said to them in chapter 15 verse 15, 'all things that I have heard of my Father I have made known unto you'. However, He now says, 'I have yet many things to say unto you, but ye cannot bear them now'. The many things are predominantly connected to chapter 16 verse 15, where He said, 'All things that the Father hath are mine: therefore said I, that he shall take of mine, and shall shew it unto you'. This is reminiscent of when the bride was on her way to meet Isaac in Genesis chapter 24. The unnamed servant showed to the bride the wealth that the father had given to Isaac. No doubt, too, the Comforter would give them a deeper understanding of the many things He had already taught them, but the Spirit of God would enable them to appreciate these 'all things' in a fuller way, by giving them the capacity to understand.

'Bear' has the idea of the bearing of a burden. The same word is used in chapter 19 verse 17, 'he bearing his cross went forth'. Divine truth was a burden to be borne, for which support was required, and the Spirit of truth would be the power to bear this burden.

'Howbeit when he, the Spirit of truth, is come, he will guide you into all truth: for he shall not speak of himself; but whatsoever he shall hear, that shall he speak: and he will shew you things to come', v. 13

'He' is emphatic. As the 'Spirit of truth', He is the one who communicates the truth of God to the disciple. As the Spirit of truth, He has taken the place of the absent one, who could say when He was here, 'I am the truth' about the Father. The Spirit of truth would show them things about the Father in the Son's absence. In chapter 17 verse 17, He says to the Father, 'thy word is truth'. The Spirit of truth and the word of truth go together. Any apprehension of divine truth can only be ours as we are guided and led by the Spirit of truth, for it is not in the natural

125

man to apprehend it. He gives the capacity for anyone at any time to apprehend the truth of God in its entirety.

The idea in the word 'guide' is that He shall lead the way into divine truth. In fact, the definite article is employed here, so the Saviour actually said, 'he will guide you into all the truth'. This means the truth in its entirety. He would give them an understanding of the deep things of God, all the truth that would result from our Lord's death, resurrection and exaltation to the Father, as it concerned them. He is thinking in terms of what is contained in the word of God. The Father spoke to the Spirit and the Spirit, in turn, spoke to the apostles the divine revelation that is given to us in the New Testament scriptures.

'For he shall not speak of himself' means that He shall not speak 'from himself'. It is the same word in chapter 15 verse 4, where 'the branch cannot bear fruit of itself', or 'from itself'. There is, certainly, unfolded to us in Romans chapter 8 and 1 Corinthians chapter 12 truth concerning the Spirit of God, but here the word means that He shall not speak 'from himself'. This means that He never speaks or acts independently of the Father and so He is to us today the perfect expression of that one will of God.

'Whatsoever he shall hear, that shall he speak'. There are communications, therefore, between divine persons. The Father speaks to the Spirit and the Spirit, in turn, speaks to us. Some people are inclined to forget this. Of course, there is a difference between the Spirit speaking to the apostles in the context of John chapter 16 and His speaking to us. When He spoke to the apostles, it was a matter of divine revelation, but when He speaks to us it is a matter of divine interpretation, as there are no new revelations today. The faith has been once for all delivered to the saints. The Spirit's work in our hearts is to interpret what has already been revealed.

The question might arise as to the need for the Father to speak to the Spirit who, as a divine person, knows all things. When the Son was here, He was on a mission and it was in connection with that mission that the Father spoke to Him. It was not in relation to His equality to the Father but as the sent one. So here, it is not the Spirit in relation to the deity of

His person but the place He takes relating to His mission, being sent to the disciples. Therefore, it is to do with His position and not His person.

'And he will show you things to come' or, more literally, 'the things to come', the whole future. He would guide them into all truth as it concerned them in relation to the fact that the Son was going back to the Father; but in respect of things to come it was not so much truth concerning them but prophetic matters such as we have in the book of Revelation.

We cannot know these things apart from God's word. God has nothing to tell men today outside of His word and so anything that is not contained in His word we must reject. The faith has been once for all delivered to the saints.

'He shall glorify me: for he shall receive of mine, and shall shew it unto you', v. 14

In 'He shall glorify me' we learn that Christ is the subject of the ministry of the Spirit. When the Son was here, He glorified the Father, so that He could say to Him in chapter 17 verse 4, 'I have glorified thee on the earth'. The Son is now speaking of the Spirit, who would come when He was absent. The Spirit now glorifies the Son.

He would glorify Him in that 'he shall receive of mine, and shall shew it unto you'. The Spirit would announce to the disciples all that is Christ's. Verse 15 amplifies this. What the Spirit would shew to them would not be limited to Jewish expectations in relation to their Messiah on an earthly throne, but it would be in relation to all things that the Father had given to the Son.

'All things that the Father hath are mine: therefore said I, that he shall take of mine, and shall shew it unto you', v. 15

The Spirit revealed to the apostles, and interprets to us, truth connected to both the Father and the Son. Keeping it in the context of this chapter, the significance of the phrase 'all things that the Father hath are mine' is to be carefully noted. All that the disciples were really

127

looking for was the Lord God giving unto Him, as the Messiah, the throne of His father David, Luke 1. 32. Now, however, as having gone back to the Father, He has given Him all things that are now connected with a glorified Christ. Every divine truth and all divine purpose centres in the Son.

The Godhead is involved in this verse, the Father, the Son and the Holy Spirit.

'A little while, and ye shall not see me: and again, a little while, and ye shall see me, because I go to the Father', v. 16

In verses 16 to 22, the Lord is speaking of a new revelation that would be theirs consequent to His resurrection. In the upper room five of the disciples had spoken to Him but since they had left it, and He was speaking of another Comforter, they said nothing. Now, as He speaks about Himself, they begin to discuss these matters with each other.

There is an important difference between the two words for 'see' that are employed in this verse. 'A little while, and ye shall not see me' refers to the time when His body was in the tomb. The word, *theōreō*, means 'ye shall not behold me', which has a deeper significance than that He would be simply out of sight. It means that He would no longer be beheld as He had been during those three-and-a-half years, when little by little they beheld some manifestation of the Son to themselves. 'Behold' means 'to be a spectator with a view to giving attention'. It is used of bodily sight and it assumes that the object is actually present. It is also used of a prolonged or continual looking or beholding.

He employs a different word in, 'again, a little while and ye shall see me'. This word, *optomai*, involves more than the eye of sense; it involves the eye of faith. They would see Him in resurrection first of all, but this word indicates that seeing Him would extend until His appearing. He showed himself for forty days to His disciples' physical eyes so that He might become to them a continual object for the eye of faith.

They would not behold Him when He lay in the tomb as they had beheld Him during those three-and-a-half years, but, when He was raised again, He would be seen not just by the eye of sense but, meaningfully, to the eye of faith. This would extend right on until His appearing. Accordingly, it may be that 'ye shall not behold me' is beholding with the physical eye while 'ye shall see' involves more than that; it is the sight of the mind, in terms of apprehension, seeing Him by faith. Today, we have an enlarged apprehension of the Saviour compared with what they beheld of Him while He was here.

The Lord's going away – being with the Father, vv. 17-33

'Then said some of his disciples among themselves, What is this that he saith unto us, A little while, and ye shall not see me: and again, a little while, and ye shall see me: and, Because I go to the Father?' v. 17

'Among themselves' has the sense of one to another. The disciples had two difficulties in their minds. The first concerns the Lord speaking of 'a little while' not beholding (*theōreō*) and 'a little while' seeing (*optomai*). The second relates to 'Because I go the Father'.

The word translated 'saith', *legō*, in 'What is this that he saith unto us' is a different verb from 'saith', *laleō*, at the end of verse 18. In verse 17, the significance is, 'What is the purpose of His saying these things?' but in verse 18, the significance is, 'What is the form in which He is conveying it to us?'

'They said therefore, What is this that he saith, A little while? we cannot tell what he saith', v. 18

In asking this question they were asking, 'What is the purpose of His saying this?' They could not tell what He said in the form in which it was conveyed.

'Now Jesus knew that they were desirous to ask him, and said unto them, Do ye inquire among yourselves of that I said, A little while, and ye shall not see me: and again, a little while, and ye shall see me?' v. 19

Jesus knew, or perceived, that they were desirous to ask Him about what He said in verse 16, and repeats it. 'Perceive' is sometimes used of natural powers of observation and sometimes of a supernatural knowledge. It may be that is the case here, that the Lord Jesus read their hearts though He also observed their expressions and heard their words.

'Verily, verily, I say unto you, That ye shall weep and lament, but the world shall rejoice: and ye shall be sorrowful, but your sorrow shall be turned into joy', v. 20

Weeping and lamenting are outward manifestations of grief. How true this was. The Lord knew that, in chapter 20, Mary would stand 'without at the sepulchre weeping' and speaks of it here. Also, in Luke chapter 23 verse 27, 'there followed him a great company of people, and of women, which also bewailed and lamented him'.

However, 'the world shall rejoice' because they thought that they had cleared the one who was disturbing their way of life. He is not using 'the world' in its universal sense but the world in contrast to 'ye'.

'And ye shall be sorrowful' or 'grieved'. Sorrow and grief have to do with inward feeling whereas weeping and lamenting are an outward expression. It began with what was outward, weeping and lamenting, and became a fixed inward feeling, in the sense of sorrow and grief. The Lord does not mention perplexity because He is speaking of what their condition was rather than its cause.

Their sorrow would not be so much because of the fear of the Jews and the persecution they would bring on them but by reason of the fact that the Messiah, upon whom they had pinned their hopes, was dead and they could not see Him. His body was in the grave. Their joy would come when they saw Him again.

'Your sorrow shall be turned into joy'. Initially, in Luke chapter 24 verse 41, it says that 'they believed... not for joy' and later, in verse 52, 'they... returned to Jerusalem with great joy'. In John chapter 20 verse 20, the disciples were 'glad, when they saw the Lord'. In verse 22, He told them that that this joy would go on, as it does and will do until we see Him at His return.

We partake of that joy in a particular way. 1 Peter chapter 4 verse 13 says, 'But rejoice, inasmuch as ye are partakers of Christ's sufferings; that, when his glory shall be revealed, ye may be glad also with exceeding joy'. When His glory is revealed, in a future day, our gladness shall be exceeding gladness. Of course, He comes **to** us today, apart from His coming **for** us in the future, for He is coming to us by the Spirit, making our hearts glad.

'A woman when she is in travail hath sorrow, because her hour is come: but as soon as she is delivered of the child, she remembereth no more the anguish, for joy that a man is born into the world', v. 21

'Anguish' is 'affliction'. This is a figure of speech that is used in God's word, in such chapters as Isaiah chapter 66 and Hosea chapter 13, but the Lord is applying it here to the disciples' particular experience. The idea is sudden sorrow by reason of His being crucified and then the sudden change to joy by reason of His being raised to them again, as verse 22 makes clear.

'Born into the world' carries with it the significance of being born into the sphere where they have to do with God.

'And ye now therefore have sorrow: but I will see you again, and your heart shall rejoice, and your joy no man taketh from you', v. 22

'Ye now therefore have sorrow' answers to the anguish of the woman in verse 21; the rest of the verse answers to the time when the travail would be over and they would see him again. 'Now' they have grief but this grief would depart; they would subsequently know joy that will

131

never depart, for no man will take it from them. No doubt their enemies would try to rob them of their joy, but they would not be successful.

It is not them seeing Him that will give them joy so much as Him seeing them. In verses 16, 17 and 19, He says, 'ye shall see me', but in verse 22, 'I will see you'. This would be the cause of all their joy.

'And in that day ye shall ask me nothing. Verily, verily, I say unto you, Whatsoever ye shall ask the Father in my name, he will give it you', v. 23

In verses 23 to 28, their future interests before the Father would be secure in the Saviour. He speaks of their requests to the Father in verse 23 and revelation from the Father in verse 25.

'In that day ye shall ask [*erōtaō*, demand] me nothing'. He would no longer be with them, by their side, and so in that day they would enquire nothing of Him. They would then ask, *aiteō*, in terms of lowly petition. The day to which He refers is this day of grace, this day of the Holy Spirit. He is now dealing with the difference between Messiah present on the earth with His people, on the one hand, and the Son now with the Father in virtue of His accomplished redemption, the Comforter come and His Father's heart revealed, on the other. They would now have access to the Father.

The two words 'Verily, verily' in John's Gospel are always to do with the introduction of a new thought or subject.

This verse may be understood either in terms of the disciples asking 'in my name' or the Father giving 'in my name'. Both would be true. 'In my name' is not just a mere formula. As we have already observed, asking in His name implies His absence but also the fact that if we do anything in anyone's name we do it as their representative. This is, in fact, what asking in His name means. Now that the Son is no longer here, we are given the Son's place before the Father. This is the wonder of the prayer of God's people today and is why we cry, 'Abba, Father', just as the Son did when He was here. However, if it should be understood that it is the

Father giving in His name, it has the significance of the Father giving in virtue of the name, which means that He is honouring His Son.

There are those who believe that worship and prayer is to the Father and to God alone. They base it on the premise that the Son was worshipped when He was here and He is worshipped in heaven, but not during this present age, and, therefore, that all worship should be to the Father. The following verses are often quoted in support. 'The hour cometh, and now is, when the true worshippers shall worship the Father in spirit and in truth: for the Father seeketh such to worship him. God is a Spirit: and they that worship him must worship him in spirit and in truth', John 4. 23, 24. 'For we are the circumcision, which worship God', Phil. 3. 3.

It cannot be denied that the general teaching of the New Testament is that worship is addressed to God the Father and the exception, rather than the general rule, is to address the Lord. If we keep this in mind it saves us to going to either extreme of teaching that you only address God or that, practically exclusively, you address the Lord. We should avoid either extreme. There are instances of the Lord being addressed. Stephen said, 'Lord Jesus, receive my spirit', Acts 7. 59. Paul refers to the fact that he besought the Lord three times in 2 Corinthians chapter 12 verse 8. There is also worship to the Lord. In Romans chapter 9 verse 5, Paul says, 'Whose are the fathers, and of whom as concerning the flesh Christ came, who is over all, God blessed for ever. Amen'. Again, in Revelation chapter 1 verse 17, John falls at His feet. There is danger when we seek to legislate in such a sacred matter as to whom we are to address in prayer.

We pray in the Spirit but we never address Him, neither is He presented in scripture as one to worship. The Spirit is the power in which we pray. Ephesians chapter 2 verse 18 says, 'For through him we both have access by one Spirit unto the Father'. Our access is by the Spirit, through Christ, to the Father. It is remarkable to observe that in the New Testament mention is made of 'the God of glory', Acts 7. 2, 'the Father of glory', Eph. 1. 17, 'the Lord of glory', 1 Cor. 2. 8, and 'the Spirit of glory', 1 Pet. 4. 14. There is not only reference to 'the God of glory' but also to 'the glory of God', Acts 7. 55. Again, there is not only reference to 'the Father of glory' but to 'the glory of the Father', Rom. 6. 4. In addition, there is reference not only to 'the Lord of glory' but also to 'the glory of the Lord', 2 Cor. 3 18. However, though we may read of 'the Spirit of glory' we never read of 'the glory of the Spirit', because the Spirit is never presented as an object of worship. His work is to glorify the Son, John 16. 14, and to direct our attention to the glory of the Father.

'Hitherto have ye asked nothing in my name: ask, and ye shall receive, that your joy may be full', v. 24

It is important to observe the tense of the verb in 'ask, and ye shall receive'. This sounds like an aorist imperative, but it is actually the present continuous. It is not, therefore, a single petition. He is really saying, 'Go on asking and you shall receive'. His person is the guarantee of the Father's response.

The so-called Lord's prayer of Matthew chapter 6 is not asking in His name. It is just addressing the Father in heaven. That was not a Christian prayer but this is Christian prayer. It speaks of a new relationship of acceptance before the Father that we enjoy, and we draw near as the Saviour Himself did.

'That your joy may be full'. The Lord is speaking of full and perfect joy. This comes to us as we avail ourselves of this unique privilege of asking in His name, which makes His resources available to us.

'These things have I spoken unto you in proverbs: but the time cometh, when I shall no more speak unto you in proverbs, but I shall shew you plainly of the Father', v. 25

He speaks of their requests to the Father, which would be answered, in verses 23, 24 and 26, and in verse 25 of a revelation from the Father to them. Going back to the Father, He Himself would show them plainly of the Father.

The Lord reminds them that He is speaking to them in proverbs, or allegories. This might include only verses 19 to 24, where He has

134

spoken of a woman having sorrow and that sorrow being turned to joy at the birth of a man. Of course, it may also include other allegories, such as that of the vine. The emphasis here, however, is that He has spoken to them in allegories but 'the time cometh, when I shall no more speak unto you in proverbs'. He would then speak to them plainly and without reserve. He had found it necessary to speak to them in allegories while He was here because they did not have the capacity to hear things plainly. However, after He had gone to the Father the Comforter would come and, by reason of the indwelling Holy Spirit, they would be capacitated to hear things plainly. He would then show them plainly of the Father that which they were not able to apprehend or appreciate while He was here.

'At that day ye shall ask in my name: and I say not unto you, that I will pray the Father for you', v. 26

'That day' is the day of the Holy Spirit. The different words for 'asking' and 'praying' occur frequently in John's Gospel. 'At that day ye shall ask in my name' employs the word *aiteō* which signifies an inferior supplicating a superior. However, when He says, 'I say not unto you, that I will pray the Father for you' He employs *erōtaō*, a word that signifies to speak to another on equal terms, implying familiarity. It is a beautiful thing that He does not need to pray the Father concerning us, for the simple reason the Father loves us; He does not need to be interceded to hear us or to answer our prayers.

The word here translated 'ask' is only once used of the Lord. It was used mistakenly by Martha in John chapter 11 verse 22 when she said, 'I know, that even now, whatsoever thou wilt ask of God, God will give it thee'. In every other instance in connection with the Son speaking to the Father it is the second word, here translated 'pray', that is used, indicating that the Son speaks to the Father on equal terms.

'For you' is not 'on your behalf' but 'concerning you'. There would be absolutely no need for the Son to intercede or mediate on their behalf, or in the Father's presence to support their requests, because they would personally have immediate access to the Father. The reason for this is given in verse 27, 'For the Father himself loveth you'. The Father would be shown plainly to them.

'For the Father himself loveth you, because ye have loved me, and have believed that I came out from God', v. 27

The expression 'the Father himself', rather than simply 'the Father', perhaps indicates that the Father loves them without any pleading on the part of the Son. It is for this reason that He would hear their requests.

The Greek word for 'loveth' is not the usual one, *agapao*, which expresses discerning love, so often used of the love of the Father to the Son or the love of the Son toward us. The word is *phileō*, which expresses love springing from natural relationships, such as the love of parents towards their children or husbands towards their wives. It is a strong love, though it does not so much involve the reasoning and intelligence. The reason why the Lord uses it here seems to be that it carries the thought of family love. He speaks to the disciples as being in the family.

In the phrase 'because ye have loved me' the Lord again employs *phileō*, 'because you have had affection for me'. This is the only instance in the Gospels where this word is used of the love of the disciples towards the Lord, though Peter uses it in John chapter 21. It is used in 1 Corinthians chapter 16 verse 22, 'If any man love not the Lord Jesus Christ, let him be Anathema Maranatha'.

The Lord speaks here not of the love of God towards the sinner but the love of the Father, who had affection for them because they had affection for His Son and believed that He came out from God. This is not here the faith that saves; it is the believing of a fact, the accepting by faith of the fact that He came out from being with God.

Love for the Lord Jesus is, of course, basic to divine revelation. Daniel is the seer of the Old Testament, of whom it is said that he was 'greatly beloved', Dan. 9. 23; 10. 11, 19. He had the revelation of the Old Testament concerning things to come; John, the seer of the New

136

Testament, received those wonderful revelations contained in the book of Revelation and was a 'disciple whom Jesus loved'.[2]

The love of God is always towards the world. The love of the Father is always towards His children. The love of Christ is usually connected with His church. The love of the Son is towards the individual, Gal. 2. 20. If this is kept in mind it will be seen how beautifully that thought runs throughout the New Testament.

In the phrase, 'and have believed that I came out from God', two different prepositions are employed. *Ek* is a prefix in the verb *exerchomai*, 'to come out'. '*Para*' has the idea of 'alongside' and usually has the significance of leaving a given position. He came out from alongside, *para*, the Father, indicating His deity. It is the same preposition that is used of the Spirit of truth, 'which proceedeth from [*para*] the Father', John 15. 26. John the Baptist was 'a man sent from [*para*] God', 1. 6, but he was 'sent' whereas the Lord Jesus 'came forth' from being alongside the Father. Thus, the disciples had believed in His divine mission.

'I came forth from the Father, and am come into the world: again, I leave the world, and go to the Father', v. 28

This is a summary of the Son's mission. There is involved in this His divine origin, His coming into the world and His return to the Father.

'I came forth from the Father' is His divine origin. It involves more than His self-abnegation. It is one of the verses that establishes the fact of His deity.

When the reference is to 'the Father' the emphasis is upon Him being the sent one and the mission this involved. The thought is one of mission rather than relationship. I came forth from the Father, having been sent by the Him on a specific mission.

---

[2] John 13. 23; 19. 26; 20. 2; 21. 7, 20.

In 'and am come into the world' there is involved His death and resurrection.

'Again, I leave the world, and go to the Father'. 'To' is the Greek preposition *pros*, which signifies 'towards the Father'. *Pros* is often used of the Son at this present time; He is not just with the Father, as being alongside Him or in His presence, but He is towards the Father. In proceeding towards the Father there is involved His ascension, a journey for a given purpose, which is that He would now be towards the Father. In fact, He never speaks of going to 'heaven' but of going to 'the Father'.

This is to be understood against the background of the Messianic hope and expectation of these disciples, as belonging to the nation to whom the Messiah was promised. They were looking forward to a Messiah who would come and deal with the enemies of the nation of Israel and God's enemies, establish His throne, sit upon the throne of David and reign 'from the river unto the ends of the earth', Ps. 72. 8. He now says that things are rather different. He was not at that time going to set up His kingdom here but, instead, He would leave the world and go to the Father.

The word 'leave' means 'to let alone', 'to let go from oneself' or 'to let go from one's further notice'. The Lord Jesus means that as having been rejected He is leaving the world to its own ways and desires. John chapter 1 verse 10 indicates that He was in the world that His hands had made, and the world of humanity knew Him not. 'He came unto his own, and his own received him not', John 1. 11. He came unto His own things, specifically the things of the nation of Israel. These included His own land, His own throne and His own temple, but His own people received Him not.

'His disciples said unto him, Lo, now speakest thou plainly, and speakest no proverb', v. 29

In verses 29 to 33, their confidence is won, v. 29 and their acknowledgement is achieved, v. 30. Then, in verse 33, He desires peace for them and bids them to 'be of good cheer'.

'Now are we sure that thou knowest all things, and needest not that any man should ask thee: by this we believe that thou camest forth from God', v. 30

'Sure' and 'knowest' are the same word, *eidō*, in the Greek text and it could therefore be translated, 'Now we know that thou knowest'. It involves an inward consciousness, 'now we are inwardly conscious that thou art inwardly conscious of all things'. His omniscience led to their belief; it gave them a good foundation for their faith. In chapter 21 verse 17, Peter employed two words when he said, 'Lord, thou knowest [*eidō*] all things; thou knowest [*ginosko*] that I love thee'. He says to the Lord, 'Thou knowest', in a general way, 'all things' but 'Thou knowest', intuitively, 'that I love thee'. Peter knew that the Lord could look into his heart at that moment and know that he loved Him. In fact, it is most interesting to study the different words for 'know' in John's writings.

'By this we believe that thou camest forth from God'. 'From' is the Greek preposition *apo*, signifying 'away from' God. The word used earlier, *para*, is usually used of leaving persons whereas *apo* is usually used of leaving places.

'Jesus answered them, Do ye now believe?' v. 31

'Now' is not the word that refers to a point of time but to a crisis or a particular state and the Lord is asking them whether they had yet arrived at that. It might seem strange that the Lord asks them this question after they had said in the preceding verse, 'we believe'. The reason is that they had said that they believed that He had come forth from God but He had told them far more than that. He told them that He came forth from the Father and that He was going back to the Father, but all they say is that they believed that He came forth from God. Therefore, the Lord asks them if they really believe, because they had a limited apprehension of Him as against all that He had been telling them concerning Himself.

It is amazing that in Acts chapter 1 verse 6 they asked whether He would at that time restore the kingdom again to Israel, when in fact He had told them that He was going to the Father. In Luke chapter 24 verse 21, those on the road to Emmaus told Him that they 'trusted that it had been he which should have redeemed Israel'. They had not truly believed that He was going back to the Father when they made statements of that nature.

'Behold, the hour cometh, yea, is now come, that ye shall be scattered, every man to his own, and shall leave me alone: and yet I am not alone, because the Father is with me', v. 32

'The hour cometh, yea, is now come' indicates that the conditions were now fulfilled for the event mentioned in this verse to take place. He tells them that they shall be scattered, or dispersed. It is the same word as in chapter 10 verse 12 where the Lord speaks of the wolf scattering the sheep.

'Every man to his own' is neuter plural, the significance of which is that they would be scattered every man to his own things. He had been the bond of their fellowship but He was going to leave them and they would be scattered.

The word 'alone' is a significant word, meaning solitary. 'I am not alone, because the Father is with me.' The preposition 'with' is *meta*, which means 'in association with me' or 'in proximity to me'. In verse 28, He came out from the Father and goes to the Father, and here, the Father is with Him.

The 'hour' refers to the cross. It recalls Zechariah chapter 13 verse 7, cited by Matthew and Mark, 'Awake, O sword, against my shepherd, and against the man that *is* my fellow, saith the Lord of hosts: smite the shepherd, and the sheep shall be scattered'. It is the smiting of the Shepherd on the cross that would cause the sheep of the flock to be scattered. It is true they forsook Him but this is more than their forsaking Him; this is their being scattered. The One who held them together, who was the great bond of their fellowship, was going to be smitten. He would be crucified and His body laid in the tomb. Then, they would be scattered.

The smiting of the Shepherd was under the hand of God. The disciples would think in terms of His being smitten by the people, but there is something greater involved than that. He was 'stricken, smitten of God, and afflicted', Isa. 53. 4. When they say, in Isaiah chapter 53 verse 3, 'we esteemed him not', they articulate what they thought when they saw Him on the cross and believed Him to be stricken, smitten of God and afflicted judicially because of His own false claims of Messiahship. They thought that on the cross God was dealing with an impostor. However, when He appears in glory, they will learn that He was wounded for their transgressions and not His own.

It is one of the unsolvable, inexplicable mysteries that by faith we have to accept that, though God forsook Him on the cross, yet the Father was with Him. On the cross the Lord Jesus uttered seven sayings. The first and the last sayings were addressed to the Father but the central saying, towards the end of the hours of darkness, was, 'My God, my God, why hast thou forsaken me?' When the Father is viewed as His God, it is always God in relation to Christ as man. 'Thou art my God from my mother's belly', Ps. 22. 10. It is as man for men, bearing the judgement of God against man's sins, that He was forsaken by a holy God. The relationship of Father and Son is another matter.

We must never think that when it says, 'it pleased the Lord to bruise him', Isa. 53. 10, it gave the Lord unqualified pleasure to bruise Him. We can be sure that it pained the Father in His heart to see the Son suffer as He did on the cross. Hagar said, 'Let me not see the death of the child', Gen. 21. 16. She was by no means the best of mothers but she could not bear to see her own child die. Could it have meant anything less to the heart of the Father than it did to Hagar? Jacob, when they showed to him Joseph's coat stained with blood, said, 'Joseph is without doubt rent in pieces. And Jacob rent his clothes, and put sackcloth upon his loins, and mourned for his son many days . . . I will go down into the grave unto my son mourning. Thus his father wept for him', Gen. 37. 33-35. Could it have meant anything less to the heart of the Father than it did to the heart of Jacob? When David is told that Absalom had died on the battlefield, 'the king was much moved, and went up to the chamber over the gate, and wept: and as he went, thus he said, O my son Absalom, my son, my son Absalom! would God I had died for thee,

O Absalom, my son, my son', 2 Sam. 18. 33. Could it have meant any less to the heart of the Father than it meant to the heart of David? A man or woman's dearest child is but a stranger to them compared to the exceeding dearness of the Son to the heart of the Father.

The title of Psalm 22 is 'To the chief Musician upon Aijeleth Shahar, A Psalm of David'. 'Aijeleth Shahar' is 'the hind of the morning'. In that Psalm our Lord is seen as the quiet, docile hind at the mercy of men considered as bulls, dogs, the lion and unicorns. At the commencement of the Psalm, the hind is forsaken. In Jeremiah chapter 14 verse 4, conditions of the drought are described, 'Because the ground is chapt, for there was no rain in the earth, the plowmen were ashamed, they covered their heads'. In the next verse, it says, 'Yea, the hind also calved in the field, and forsook it, because there was no grass'. The hind was acting unnaturally towards its offspring because it could not bear to see it die a slow, lingering death of starvation. God is holy, yet God could not bear to see His Hind suffer and die as He did on the cross.

'These things I have spoken unto you, that in me ye might have peace. In the world ye shall have tribulation: but be of good cheer; I have overcome the world', v. 33

'These things' are what He had spoken to them since Judas had gone out. The first application of what the Lord says here would be to the imminent experience of the disciples, in connection with His death and burial, but it has a wider significance in that it applies to us today. In the world we have tribulation but in Him we have peace, in Him our hearts can rest.

He had spoken these things unto them 'that In me ye might have peace'. This is rather different to the peace of John chapter 14 verse 27 where He said, 'Peace I leave with you, my peace I give unto you: not as the world giveth, give I unto you. Let not your heart be troubled, neither let it be afraid'. 'My peace' was His peculiar peace, the peace of undisturbed communion with the Father, the peace of an unclouded sky, but here it is, 'that in me ye might have peace', that their hearts might be at rest in the midst of tribulation.

The Lord Jesus mentions peace three times in John chapter 20. There is peace as the result of His work, v. 19, when He invites them to look on His hands. Then, there is peace connected with their mission, as He sends them out, v. 21. Then, when Thomas was present, v. 26, there is peace for the remnant in a future day. This links with Ephesians chapter 2, where peace is also mentioned three times. He has made peace, v. 15, 'having abolished in his flesh the enmity'. This refers to the giving of His flesh in death and links with showing them His hands and His side. He 'came and preached peace', v. 17, which links with the mission. Third, 'he is our peace', v. 14, peace between Jew and Gentile.

He speaks peace to His own both in John chapter 20 and Luke chapter 24. Each chapter has a different setting. In Luke chapter 24 they were afraid of Him, supposing Him to be a spirit, a phantom, v. 37. His answer to them was, 'Behold my hands and my feet, that it is I myself'. In John chapter 20, however, the fear is not because of Him but because of the Jews. Again, it says, 'He shewed unto them his hands and his side', v. 20.

'In the world ye shall have tribulation' is really 'in the world ye have tribulation'. Tribulation had already begun for them. The saints of this church age will not be here in the time of 'the tribulation' in Daniel's seventieth prophetic week. That tribulation comes as retribution at a specified hour, but tribulation as you have it in this verse is the constant experience of the disciple.

No doubt the remnant of the tribulation will have His peace. This will not be the peace of undisturbed communion, for that belongs to those who belong to the age of the Spirit, but they shall find peace and rest in Him. The world shall say, 'Peace and safety', 1 Thess. 5. 3, but then sudden destruction overcomes them. Of course, when the world says, 'peace and safety' it means peace and safety from anything that God might do to those who are sheltered by the antichrist. Conversely, the remnant in the day of tribulation find peace in the one they are expecting.

'Be of good cheer' means, 'be of good courage'. He has overcome the world. Whatever the world levelled against Him, and He had experienced treachery and shame and would experience death, He overcame the world. What causes us to overcome the world is our faith in the Son of God, 1 John 5. 5. That is the standpoint, too, of the overcomer in Revelation, whether in chapters 2 and 3 or 21.

Chapter 17

This prayer was evidently uttered on the night of our Lord's betrayal, somewhere between the upper room and the garden of Gethsemane. At the end of chapter 14, the Son of God leaves the upper room. He said, 'But that the world may know that I love the Father; and as the Father gave me commandment, even so I do. Arise, let us go hence', v. 31. In chapter 18, He passes over the brook Cedron into the garden of Gethsemane. It is, therefore, between the events of chapters 14 and 18 that the prayer of this chapter was uttered by the Lord on the night of His betrayal.

On two separate occasions that night the Son of God was seen and heard to be praying. The Lord taught, in the sermon on the mount, the wrong of praying to be seen, but God's Son never prayed to be seen and heard. If He was seen and heard to be praying it was for the spiritual enrichment of those who saw and heard Him. We would have missed so much if there was never placed on record for us the prayer of this chapter. In fact, we have in this prayer divine truth from eternity to eternity.

There is a stark contrast between the prayers on that particular night. With regard to His prayer in the garden, He speaks of His exceeding sorrow. Mark speaks of His sore amaze and great heaviness. Luke speaks of His agony. In Hebrews chapter 5, the writer speaks of Gethsemane and of our Saviour's strong crying, His tears and His fear. This was the experience of the Saviour in the garden: sorrow, agony, tears, sweat and fear. In John chapter 17, however, things are rather different. In this prayer He speaks of love, joy, and glory. He speaks of love in these terms, 'Thou lovedst me before the foundation of the world', v. 24. He speaks of joy, 'that they might have my joy fulfilled in themselves', v. 13. He speaks of glory, 'the hour is come; glorify thy son', v. 1, and 'that they may behold my glory', v. 24.

In the garden of Gethsemane, the Lord Jesus is prostrate in the dust of the earth. This is not recorded in John's Gospel. Rather, in John chapter 18, it is not the Lord Jesus who is in the dust of the earth but those who came to arrest Him. It is in the other Gospels that we find our Saviour prostrate in the dust of the earth. Matthew says, 'he went a little farther, and fell on his face', 26. 39. There, as God's Son is upon His face in sweat, tears and fear, He has on His mind the cup which He will drink during those dread hours of darkness. He is thinking of the suffering and of being made sin, of the abandonment of the tree and all that is involved in suffering 'without the gate', Heb. 13. 12. It is little wonder that He is prostrate.

John chapter 17 is rather different. He is not here prostrate in the dust of the earth but is, in fact, lifting up His eyes to heaven. The preposition is 'into' heaven rather than 'towards' heaven. He is not thinking of the cross in this prayer but of heaven and His going there. If, in verse 1, He looks into heaven, in verse 24 He is, in spirit, already there. He says, 'Father, I will that they also, whom thou hast given me, be with me where I am; that they may behold my glory'. He clearly did not mean where He was praying at that particular moment but 'where I am' in heaven; He was, even then, there in spirit.

There is a paradox in this prayer which helps us to understand it. He says, in verse 11, 'And now I am no more in the world', but, in verse 13, He says, 'these things speak I in the world'. There appears to be a contradiction. The answer to this is that in spirit He is no more in the world though physically He is still there. This is the answer to many of the problems that beset those who consider this prayer, such as whether or not it is a high priestly prayer. Physically, He was in the world, but in spirit He was already out of it.

In this connection, notice the movement of the spirit of God's Son in this prayer. In verse 4, He says, 'I have glorified thee on the earth: I have finished the work which thou gavest me to do'. In this verse, He looks back on a life that has been lived, in which He glorified the Father, and on the work that He was given to do, which He had finished. Then, in verse 11, He says, 'I am no more in the world'. Next, in verse 13, He says to the Father, 'And now come I to thee'. Finally, note verse 24, where He is now in heaven. What delightful progress this is.

It is important to observe that in this prayer the Son addresses the Father in a threefold way. In verses 1 and 5, speaking in regard to

Himself, He addresses Him as 'Father'. Then, in verse 11, speaking with particular regard to His own, He addresses Him as 'Holy Father'. Finally, in verse 25, when speaking with particular regard for the world, He addresses Him as 'righteous Father'.

Broadly speaking, this prayer divides itself into three sections. In verses 1 to 5, the Son is speaking to the Father in relation to Himself. In verses 6 to 19, He is speaking to the Father about those disciples who were then with Him, listening to the words of His prayer. Then, in verses 20 to 26, He prays first of all for those who would believe on Him through the testimony of those men who were with him and then goes beyond those to embrace the whole church, v. 24.

In verses 1 to 5, when He speaks to the Father in relation to Himself the subject is that of glory.

In verses 6 to 19, when He speaks to the Father about the disciples, those who were then listening to Him, He firstly tells the Father what He Himself had been doing for them while He was with them. Then, He expresses to the Father what He desires the Father to do for them. In fact, He wants the Father to do for them what He Himself had been doing for them. He had kept them in the Father's name and He now wanted the Father to keep them in His name, in the enjoyment of Himself as Father.

In verses 20 to 26, when He speaks to the Father about those who would believe on Him through the testimony of those who were then with Him, and also for the whole church, He prays in respect of their oneness. In respect of those who would believe, He prays that they would be 'one in us': one in love and affection, one in aim, one in object. This was beautifully fulfilled in the book of Acts in such things as the fact that they continued steadfastly, they were all together in one place, they had all things in common, and great grace was upon them all. It was impossible that a prayer of God's Son would not be fulfilled. They were one in the Father's love and affection, one in fellowship and in prayer, one in aim and in purpose.

147

When He prays in relation to the whole church, however, this is again to do with oneness; not now oneness in the Father and the Son in terms of love and fellowship, aim and object but that they might be one in manifested glory. That has not yet been fulfilled but all the saints shall be perfected in one in manifested glory at our Saviour's appearing. Notice, too, that the oneness in Acts chapter 2 had in view 'that the world may believe' but the oneness in manifested glory has in view that the world 'may know'. When they are manifested with the Saviour, perfected in one in manifested glory, it will be too late for the world to believe but it shall then know.

Himself – glory, vv. 1-5

'These words spake Jesus, and lifted up his eyes to heaven, and said, Father, the hour is come; glorify thy Son, that thy Son also may glorify thee', v. 1

In verses 1 to 5, he speaks to the Father in relation to Himself.

'These words spake Jesus' refers to what He has just been saying to His disciples and now He turns to speak to His Father. In doing so He lifts up His eyes to the Father. The preposition is not just 'to' heaven or 'towards' heaven; the word means 'into' heaven. As the Son of God, He did not need to look into heaven, for He is all seeing and omniscient, but here is Jesus, a man on earth, looking up into heaven. The publican in Luke chapter 18 would not lift up his eyes to heaven in view of all that was in his breast but here is one in whose breast was nothing to offend God. By way of contrast, in Him there was everything that pleased God.

We cannot now look into heaven but, to faith, the thought of Him being there is very real. Faith is the evidence of things not seen. Roman Catholicism needs a crucifix with a body on it, which is all to do with sight, but faith is deeper than that as it is the evidence of things not seen. God's Son is doing something, therefore, that we could not really do.

Reverence of heart will cause us to have a reverent posture in prayer. Daniel went on his knees three times a day. Solomon fell on his knees at the dedication of the temple and lifted his heart to heaven. Paul fell on his knees when speaking with the Ephesian elders. Our Lord fell on His knees in the garden. Paul bowed his knees unto the Father, in whom every family in heaven and earth is named. Thus, while the emphasis is on having the right spirit, this will result in bowing the knee whenever possible. The idea of standing for prayer is connected with public prayer.

There are many 'hours' in this Gospel. In chapter 2, it is the hour of His manifested glory when He shall turn Israel's water into wine. In chapter 12, it is the hour of His suffering. In this verse, it is the hour of His being glorified in heaven. Here is an hour that is unique in the annals of time. A man says to the Father that the hour is come for Him to be glorified. He was the only one who could say, 'I have glorified thee on the earth'. We shall be glorified on the principle of pure and undeserved grace, but, in Acts chapter 3 verse 21, Peter says regarding the Saviour, 'Whom the heaven must receive'. It was a 'must' that the heavens would receive Jesus. Here was a man in whom is no sin, who was never morally unfit for heaven.

In the opening verses, the Son makes an impersonal approach, but in verse 5 it is different. Notice, in verse 1, the references to 'thy Son', but in verse 5 it is a personal approach, 'glorify thou me'. The reason for this is that in the opening verses He approaches the Father as the subject Son and the glory for which He prays is an acquired glory. It is the answer for all that the subject Son had done for the Father here on earth. In verse 5, when He speaks in a personal way, the glory about which He prays is not an acquired glory but rather that which is His essentially and eternally. In verse 1, he prays with the intimacy of communion, but in verse 5 he prays with equality.

The glory of God is the expression of the collective attributes of God in a person, God's Son. Of course, there is glory such as His creatorial glory and the glory of His grace. Creatorial glory is the expression of His inward power. The glory of His grace is the expression of his inward love. In glorifying His Son, God showered honour and glory upon Him, an acquired glory rather than that which is essential and eternal. It is important to distinguish these things. The glory of verse 22 is the same as the glory of verse 1 and He is going to share it with us. In verse 24, however, it is a glory that He cannot share, for it is His divine and essential glory, which we shall behold.

'As thou hast given him power over all flesh, that he should give eternal life to as many as thou hast given him', v. 2

The connection between verses 1 and 2 is to be noted. In verse 1, the Son prays that the Father might glorify Him in heaven. The Son intended that once He was glorified in heaven, He would continue to glorify the Father by giving eternal life to as many as the Father had given to Him. The Father has given His Son authority to do this. His desire to glorify the Father remained the same and He does this by giving eternal life to as many as the Father has given Him. The Father is glorified in this because His people, having eternal life, know the Father and the Son.

The word 'power' is 'authority' and here it is authority in relation to blessing, namely that He should give eternal life to as many as the Father has given Him. It must be remembered that the Father has given the Son authority over all flesh, both saved and unsaved, regenerate and unregenerate. There can be no limitation in terms of all flesh; it simply means 'all mankind'. That authority involves two matters. In respect of those who are the love gift to the Son, it involves blessing, but in respect of those who are unregenerate and outside of that company it must involve judgement.

His authority in the matter of blessing and judgement is summed up in John chapter 5. Both are connected with His words. In verse 25, there is the exercise of His authority today. Those who are spiritually dead shall live when they hear His voice, and no one has life who does not have that experience of hearing the authoritative voice of the Son of God. If the authority of the voice of the Son of God in quickening is heard in verse 25, the authoritative voice of the Son of man, in the future, is heard in the matter of raising and judgement, in verse 28.

His authority in Hebrews chapter 2, which tells us that all things shall be put under the feet of the Son of man, is to be distinguished. There it is the authority of the Son of man over all creation but, in this verse, it is over all mankind. His authority in Matthew chapter 28, where He says 'All power [authority] is given unto me', means that He has authority over every opposing force in heaven and on earth that would array itself against His people in the carrying out of His commission. Then, in Revelation chapter 1 verse 18, He has authority over death and hell.

Power and authority are two different words. Authority is something that is vested in the individual, but power is the exercise of that authority. A policeman might be out on the street, having all the authority that is necessary to arrest an unruly man, but he might not have the power to do it. God's Son, however, is not only invested with authority but He has the power to exercise that authority when He wills.

This prayer anticipates Calvary and His resurrection, and the authority to give eternal life was given to Him in resurrection. It is not the same idea as in 1 Corinthians chapter 15, where the second man is a life-giving spirit. It is on the other side of death that He gives eternal life and so He gives eternal life as a risen man. 'For the wages of sin is death; but the gift of God is eternal life through Jesus Christ our Lord', Rom. 6. 23. The word used is not 'through' but 'in' Christ Jesus our Lord. That is, the eternal life that we have today is in Christ Jesus our Lord, the risen and exalted man at God's right hand. There is, therefore, a contrast between everlasting life in the Old Testament and everlasting life now. In the Old Testament, in Psalm 133 and Daniel chapter 12, it is everlasting life in connection with the earth and the millennial reign, but the everlasting life that we enjoy now is heavenly in its character, as it is in Christ Jesus our Lord.

Eternal life may be summarized as follows. It was **promised** before the world began, a command speaking of divine authority in respect of the fact that man should enjoy it. It was essentially and eternally in the Son, 'in him was life', John 1. 4. It was **manifested** at His incarnation; 1 John chapter 1 verse 2 speaks of 'that eternal life, which was with the Father, and was manifested unto us', namely to the apostles, after our Saviour's incarnation. It **comes to us** only consequent upon His death; Romans chapter 5 verse 21 says, 'That as sin hath reigned unto death, even so might grace reign through righteousness unto eternal life by Jesus Christ our Lord'. It is **secured** for man through Him at God's right hand, Rom. 6. 23. It is **obtained** through believing, John 3. 16. John chapter 6 verse 54 says that, 'Whoso eateth my flesh, and drinketh my blood, hath eternal life', meaning that by faith they appropriated the benefits of His death. It is something that is **offered** to 'whosoever'. Also, in John chapter 10, it is His sheep who **receive** eternal life. This is an amazing statement; sheep receive it, and there are few things so defenceless as sheep. Then, in John chapter 17, those who receive it are those who are the Father's love gift to the Son.

When the Bible speaks of eternal life it is not just thinking in terms of ceaseless existence. In fact, the word 'life' in the expression 'eternal life' is not the word that simply means existence. Also, whilst the word 'eternal' is sometimes used in relation to time and what is temporal, it means more than that. The apostle says, 'While we look not at the things which are seen, but at the things which are not seen: for the things which are seen are temporal; but the things which are not seen are eternal', 2 Cor. 4. 18. 'Eternal' here means something that is above time and space, something that is connected with God and with the life of heaven. It is the quality of the life and not the duration of it. The word 'life', therefore, means much more than just existence and 'eternal' is far more than a contrast with time.

Sinners are spoken of as being 'dead in trespasses and sins', Eph. 2. 1. They are not viewed as being diseased or dying but as dead. They are as a lifeless corpse or a sapless tree and devoid of any living principle Godward. But now sinners have eternal life through believing. There is now a living principle Godward and we know God and His Son. The moment a person believes, he has everlasting life. 'He that hath the Son hath life', 1 John 5. 12. To have the Son now as a personal Saviour is to have life but we shall have it in all its fullness in heaven's glory, where it properly belongs.

152

The source of the gift is God but the Son is the one who dispenses it, and He dispenses it to those who are the Father's love gift to Him, 'as many as thou hast given him'. These are quickened by the Holy Spirit. There are those who suggest that we were given to Him away back in eternity, but the Father's love gift to the Son was of men out of this world, which seems to suggest that they were given in time. I believe that I was given to the Son by the Father the moment that I received eternal life. Notice again the impersonal way in which He speaks to the Father when He says, 'As thou hast given him power over all flesh'. He is not approaching the Father as the eternal Son but as the subject Son and thus we have a gift to the subject Son, which must relate to time.

The truth of being chosen in Christ before the foundation of the world, as stated in Ephesians chapter 1 verse 4, belongs to eternity but the work of Christ was necessary to make that possible. My trust in Christ through the operation of the Spirit was also necessary. Eternal purpose and the working out of eternal purpose are to be distinguished. In 1 Peter chapter 1 verse 2, the foreknowledge of God the Father is eternal, but it is worked out now through the sanctification of the Spirit unto the obedience of faith. Thus, they were the Father's in eternity and the Father gave them to the Son the moment they received eternal life. Of course, it would be true to say that in divine purpose there was a *fait accomplit*, although, in experience, it was the moment I received eternal life. There are two sides to this: there is that which is viewed from the divine standpoint; and that which is viewed from the standpoint of the working out of divine counsel. In terms of Romans chapter 8 verses 29 and 30, we are foreknown, predestinated, called, justified, and already glorified. This is not as far as our experience is concerned but from the divine standpoint it is a *fait accomplit*.

At Calvary He paid a price for all mankind, but not all mankind is going to be saved. He gave himself a ransom for all, but all will not be saved. However, those are saved whom the Father gives to the Son. This is the distinction between propitiation and substitution. The same is in John chapter 3 verse 16. God loved the world but eternal life only becomes the possession of those who believe.

'And this is life eternal, that they might know thee the only true God, and Jesus Christ, whom thou hast sent', v. 3

Life eternal is not merely life in terms of duration but in terms of its quality and character. Life is a real thing, connected with a living, personal, intimate knowledge. The Father is glorified, in that being in possession of eternal life given to us by the Son we know both the Father and His Son. Without this eternal life we could not know God and Jesus Christ the sent one.

Of course, full knowledge cannot be a thing we possess down here. In Ephesians chapter 3 verse 19, Paul speaks of knowing the love of Christ which cannot be fully known, of apprehending the incomprehensible. In Philippians chapter 3 verse 10, Paul's resolve was, 'That I may know him', which is the high-water level of Christian experience but, again, it does not involve full and complete knowledge. God has revealed himself in His word and we only know God as He is revealed in His word.

In eternity we will not know everything at one time and our position then be static. There will be an increasing, progressive knowledge of the Son and the Father to all eternity as fresh and increasing revelations are given to us. We can look forward to knowing things that are not now revealed regarding God's Son. There will be no change in respect of the quality of eternal life; that quality is to know but our enjoyment of it will increase.

Our degree of knowledge then will depend on how much we have learned of Him now, which will be the start point in eternity. The more we get to know Him now the greater will be our increasing knowledge of Him then. We must not think that when we get into His presence we shall all know Him eternally in exactly the same way. It begins here, and though there are conditions down here that militate against an increasing knowledge of Christ there will be no such conditions in heaven. The meaning of the word manna is, 'What is it?' This aptly speaks of our Saviour. As the question relates to Him, there will not be a full answer to it to all eternity. We shall be saying continually in eternity, 'What is it?' It must be remembered that 'no man knoweth the Son, but the Father', Matt. 11. 27.

John speaks generally of eternal life as a present possession, whereas Paul speaks of laying hold of eternal life, a progressive thing. As eternity proceeds, eternal life will become more enjoyable. When a child is born it has life, but that child does not know anything about it. As the child develops, however, his life is enjoyed. It is the same with eternal life, which grows and increases in knowledge and apprehension. We are all saved on the basis of the same work but we all have a different apprehension. There would be little point in laying hold of eternal life if in eternity we were all going to be the same.

Also, on earth in the millennium, people will not have the same appreciation. The nations of those who are saved will not have the same appreciation as the nation of Israel. Even within the church, and amongst angels, there will be variety and so there will be a variety in heaven and on earth. In the millennium, too, there are different positions in manifested glory as we reign with Christ. In the eternal state, we shall continue to be associated with Him. We shall not then be reigning over the earth in positions of glory, for He will not then be reigning as King, but we shall know Him as a bride with a husband, enjoying all His love.

Consideration must be given as to why it is 'the only true God' and 'Jesus Christ, whom thou hast sent'. In Matthew chapter 16, the 'living God' is seen in contrast to the 'gates of hell'; the gates of hell cannot prevail against the Son of the living God. Here, however, it is the 'true God', in clear contrast to 'false gods'. There might be involved in this the thought of Jew and Gentile. For the Gentile, He is the only true God; in Thessalonica they 'turned to God from idols to serve the living and true God', 1 Thess. 1. 9. What the Jew needed to understand, however, was that Jesus Christ was the sent one, something which at first the Jew refused to understand and accept. Perhaps these two things are in view: the only true God for the heathen; and Jesus Christ, the sent one, for the Jew.

The word 'true' in Jesus' statement, 'he that sent me is true', John 7. 28, is not always in contrast to what is false. It also has the significance of what is true in contrast to what is partial. In the Old Testament, God was revealed in many parts and in many manners but now it is the 'true God' in complete revelation. This is the idea in John chapter 7. God's Son is that one person in the Godhead by whom the glory of deity is revealed. He alone is the brightness of God's glory and the express image of His person. Everything about God is true and is in contrast to everything that is either false or imperfectly revealed.

In 1 John chapter 5 verse 20, the statement, 'This is the true God, and eternal life', relates to Christ in His essential deity. There, it is not eternal life 'in Him' but, rather, He is the eternal life in all the wonder of His deity. Eternal life which we have 'in Him' now is not in Him as the true God but as the risen and exalted man. This is in line with Romans chapter 6 verse 23.

'I have glorified thee on the earth: I have finished the work which thou gavest me to do', v. 4

There is little difficulty in the statement, 'I have glorified thee on the earth'. A question arises, however, as to whether the statement 'I have finished the work which thou gavest me to do' relates to Calvary in view of the fact that it was not yet experientially an accomplished fact.

I take it that in this verse we have both our Lord's life and death. He glorified the Father in the life that He lived on earth, where the Father had been so dishonoured, and He finished the work which the Father gave Him to do. He speaks here as if Calvary was an accomplished fact, just as He speaks in verse 24 as if He were already glorified, when He said, 'Father, I will that they also, whom thou hast given me, be with me where I am'. He was, in spirit, already in heaven. In like manner in this verse, in spirit His life had been lived and His work had been completed.

In John chapter 5 verse 36, the Saviour spoke of 'the works which the Father hath given me to finish' but here it is not the 'works' but the 'work'. The 'works' of chapter 5 would include his miracles but in

156

chapter 17 it is the 'work'. I take it that He is referring to Calvary, which was not a work which He Himself chose but the work that the Father gave Him to do and which He, the Son, finished.

The Apostle Paul could say, 'I have fought a good fight, I have finished my course, I have kept the faith', 2 Tim. 4. 7. Wonderful as this was, it falls very far short of what was true of the Son of God. Uniquely, He could say, 'I have glorified thee on the earth: I have finished the work which thou gavest me to do'.

'And now, O Father, glorify thou me with thine own self with the glory which I had with thee before the world was', v. 5

There are important distinctions between verse 1 and verse 5. In verse 1, He says, 'glorify thy Son', an impersonal approach, but, in verse 5, He says, 'glorify thou me', a personal approach. In verse 1, He prays in respect of an acquired glory, which was the Father's answer to all the glory that the Son brought to Him when He was here, but, in verse 5, He prays in respect of His divine and essential glory. This is 'the glory which I had with thee before the world was'. In verse 1, He prays with the intimacy of communion, but, in verse 5, it is the intimacy of equality, that He might resume the position He had occupied along with the Father to all eternity.

It is the subject Son here who is praying on earth but he speaks to the Father regarding His being glorified with the glory that is His by right as the eternal Son. It must be remembered in respect of our Lord's glorification and exaltation that God has given to Him as a risen and exalted man what was always true of Him as God. In Ephesians 1 verses 20 and 21, for example, God has set him down at His own right hand in a position far above all, which was always true of Him but is now true of Him as a risen and exalted man.

'Glorify thou me' is spoken by the subject Son, who has now gone back to heaven, resuming a position that He left. He shares equally with the Father, as a subject Son, all that glory in a position that is proper to it, which belongs exclusively to deity. It is the Ark of the covenant in the holy of holies, the shittim wood overlaid within and without with gold.

157

The verse becomes simplified for us in the *New Translation* of J. N. DARBY, 'and now glorify me, thou Father, along with thyself, with the glory which I had along with thee before the world was'. The thought is not that the Son would resume His divine and eternal and essential glory, for He never left it, but that He would resume the position that was proper to it. That position is 'along with the Father'.

This does not mean that at His incarnation the Son 'left' or 'laid aside' His divine, eternal and essential glory nor, of course, that He laid aside His deity. There was no interruption in His divine and eternal glory but there was an interruption in His occupying the position that was proper to it. It might be better to say that He 'veiled his glory' but, according to this verse, He laid aside the position proper to that eternal glory. In verse 4, He says, 'I have glorified thee **on the earth**', and now, in verse 5, 'Father, glorify thou me **[along] with thine own self**'. The earth was not the proper sphere for the divine and essential glory; that sphere was 'along with thine own self'. In verse 8, He says, 'I came out from thee', which has the thought that 'I came out from being with thee'. This is how John's Gospel begins, 'the word was with God', and also John's first Epistle, 'that eternal life, which was with the Father'. 'With God' and 'with the Father' was a position proper to His divine glory and He now asks that that position may be resumed.

In Philippians chapter 2, the glory that is His is a glory that answers to the depths to which He went. He 'became obedient unto death . . . Wherefore God also hath highly exalted him'. The glory that is given Him there is a glory such that things celestial, terrestrial, and infernal shall bow the knee and acknowledge that He is Lord. Here, however, it is rather the private side to it.

'Glory' has a very broad sense and is hard to define. There is creatorial glory, the glory of God's grace, His divine and essential glory, His moral glory and there are so many other aspects of glory. His eternal and essential glory is the complete expression of all the attributes of God. John is the writer who tells us what God is: 'God is spirit', John 4. 24 JNDmg.; 'God is light', 1 John 1. 5; and 'God is love', 4. 8. In John chapter 1 verse 14, 'we beheld his glory'; the glory that they saw was grace and truth. In a scene of evil, grace is the activity of love, and truth is the activity of light. Apart from time and space, God is light and love, but, when God's Son came into the world of evil, light became truth and love became grace.

The glory of verse 24 is connected with the Father's house whereas the glory of verse 22 is His millennial glory that He shall share with us.

The significance of the expression 'before the world was' is simply that the glory which He had was before time and apart from the creation of the world, before the introduction of man. In verse 24, the expression is, 'before the foundation of the world'. Thus, to all eternity He shared with the Father all the glory of deity and was the object of the Father's love. In 1 Peter chapter 1 verse 20, He is the lamb who was verily foreknown 'before the foundation of the world', though this is not so much connected with glory as with divine purpose.

The disciples – kept, vv. 6-19

'I have manifested thy name unto the men which thou gavest me out of the world: thine they were, and thou gavest them me; and they have kept thy word', v. 6

In verses 6 to 19 the Son of God prays particularly for those disciples with whom He had been in the world.

We can only feebly conceive the impact which must have been made on the minds of those disciples to hear the Son pray for them as 'the men which thou gavest me out of the world: thine they were, and thou gavest them me'. These men listen to the Son speaking to the Father about eternal and divine counsel that they would never otherwise have known.

He manifested the Father's name in His teaching and example while He was here on earth. Moving among the disciples He was teaching them by example in order to make God known to them as Father. Israel, nationally, knew God as Father, Mal. 1. 6, and, also, something about

159

sonship.[3] However, there is now something different in that God is their Father individually rather than in a collective way.

'The men which thou gavest me out of the world' is a wonderful statement concerning the Father's love gift to the Son. These men were the gift; not only were they 'men' but they were men 'out of the world'. We would not have been surprised if God had given to His Son angels from the realms of glory, but the Father's love gift to the Son was men out of this world, the world into which sin had entered and where men were in the steel grip of the enemy. 'Behold I and the children which God hath given me', Heb. 2. 13.

'Thine they were' is in the sense of Romans chapter 8 verse 29, 'whom he did foreknow', also chosen 'in him before the foundation of the world', Eph. 1. 4, and 'Elect according to the foreknowledge of God the Father', 1 Pet. 1. 2. They were the Father's in divine, eternal counsel and electing choice before the foundation of the world. This is the sovereignty of God in salvation as a result of which it is impossible to think of anybody being lost who has been the Father's love gift to the Son.

It is humbling to think that we are the Father's love gift to His own Son. In this chapter there are seven gifts from the Father to the Son. In addition to these men, these gifts are: authority, v. 2; the work, v. 4; all things whatsoever thou hast given me, v. 7; the words, v. 8; the glory, v. 22; and my glory, v. 24. Of these seven gifts, one, the gift of men, is mentioned seven times, and the development of truth in respect of those whom the Father had given Him is fascinating.

'And they have kept thy word' might have brought a blush to the cheeks of these men as they hear the Son say this to the Father. Each one of them had failed. There were times when they had not kept the Father's word but, when the Son speaks to the Father, He never mentions their faults. The divine assessment of any man is never based on any isolated incidents. If God were to assess us on any particular failings in our lives, we should end up hopeless. Thank God, He takes account and makes

---

[3] Exod. 4. 22; Hos. 11. 1; Rom. 9. 4.

His assessment based on the whole tenor of a man's life and service. Further, in verse 10, He says, 'and I am glorified in them'.

Some suggest that 'thou gavest them me' also refers to divine counsel, but it rather seems to refer to the moment they put their trust in Christ. It was then that they were given by the Father to the Son as men out of this world.

'Now they have known that all things whatsoever thou hast given me are of thee', v. 7

'All things' is to do with His mission and the message that He had given to them. It became clear to them that His mission and His message were of His Father.

'For I have given unto them the words which thou gavest me; and they have received them, and have known surely that I came out from thee, and they have believed that thou didst send me', v. 8

'Words' is not the plural of 'word' in verse 6; different Greek words are employed. In verse 6, the word is *logos*, whereas here it is the word *rhēmata*, which means 'sayings' or 'communications'. The reference here is to those daily communications which the Son received from the Father and made known to the men which were with Him. This is the fulfilment of Isaiah chapter 50 verse 4. 'He wakeneth morning by morning, he wakeneth mine ear to hear as the learned'.

A word of warning here. It is necessary to know the word of God, the whole body of divine truth, and it is important to be instructed as to its truth. At the same time, it is important to be in receipt of daily communications from Him. It is possible to know the Bible from cover to cover yet not be in touch with heaven. It is vital to have the ear opened day by day to hear daily communications. Get to know your book, study and become instructed in it, but see to it that daily you have communications from heaven. It is possible to know the truth and handle it in a carnal way, but this will not happen when hearing such daily communications.

It is to do with the mystery of His person that at one and the same time the Lord Jesus knew all things and yet waited on daily communications from heaven as to what He should say. Luke chapter 2 verse 52 says that He 'increased in wisdom and stature'. If He was all-wise how could He increase in wisdom? The point is that as a subject Son He acted and behaved as a Son to the Father, in every sense of the word. Daily He heard from the Father. That is why He said to the devil, 'Man shall not live by bread alone, but by every word that proceedeth out of the mouth of God', Matt. 4. 4. He was saying to the devil that He could turn that stone into bread if His Father told Him to do it. In the absence of such a word from the Father, if He were to turn that stone into bread, exercising His divine power, He would have ceased to be a dependent man.

This matter is very important. The question that is asked today is, 'Could Jesus sin?' Interestingly, the question is never, 'Could the Son of God sin?' This is part of an endeavour today to think of Him as Jesus, at the expense of thinking of Him as the Son of God. This is always the aim of the devil. That temptation was directed to Him to act as God and leave his position as a dependent man. He also tempted Him to cast Himself down from the pinnacle of the temple, implying that as a dependent man God would look after Him. He urged Him to act as if He was not God. Men are still trying to divide His person.

In all of this there is a mystery that we cannot understand. The Son is inscrutable, known only by the Father. He acts as a subject Son, receiving daily communications, and yet, in chapter 13, He knew that His hour was come and that the Father had put all things into His hands. Peter says to him, 'Lord, thou knowest all things'.

The disciples had come to know that these words were from a divine source. Through these sayings that they had heard and received they knew surely that He came out from the Father and they believed that the Father sent Him. 'I came' speaks of His deity; 'thou didst send' speaks of His manhood. 'I came' indicates His love; 'thou didst send' speaks of the Father's love.

There are two words for 'send'. One, *apostellō*, is used here, whilst the other, *pempō*, is used in John chapter 20 verse 21, where He said, 'as my Father hath sent me, even so send I you'. The difference is that in John chapter 17 it was an apostolic sending whereas in John chapter 20 the idea is that the one who sends accompanies the one who is sent. Both were true of the Son. The Father sent Him officially, which is what we have in this chapter but, in John chapter 20, the Father sent Him and accompanied Him. That is how the Son sent the disciples; He sent them, but He would accompany them, working with them.

'I pray for them: I pray not for the world, but for them which thou hast given me; for they are thine', v. 9

The Lord Jesus is not seen as a supplicant in this chapter. 'I pray' is 'I demand' and He speaks to the Father as an equal.

He prays concerning them and not concerning the world. This is a priestly prayer. Some people ask how it can be a priestly prayer because 'if he were on earth, he should not be a priest', Heb. 8. 4. We have seen already that this prayer is prayed from the standpoint that He is physically here on earth but in spirit He is back with the Father. It is from that standpoint He says, 'I pray for them'. 'He ever liveth to make intercession' for us, Heb. 7. 25. His priestly intercession is always on behalf of His own and not on behalf of the world. It is the Holy Spirit who deals with the lost.

From the standpoint of the human intellect, it is not easy to understand that the Father has given them to the Son, but the Son says to the Father, 'they are thine'. The answer is found in verse 10.

'And all mine are thine, and thine are mine; and I am glorified in them', v. 10

I believe that our Saviour is here speaking in terms of preciousness. The Father had given them to His Son, but they were still the Father's, for 'all mine are thine, and thine are mine'. In John chapter 10 verses 28 and 29, His sheep are in the hands of both the shepherd and the

163

Father, out of which no man could pluck them. There it is in terms of security but here it is in terms of preciousness.

We do well to enjoy these things and remember that salvation is more than the forgiveness of sins and salvation from hell. It is eternal security and preciousness to the Father and the Son. Salvation does not depend upon our feelings but on the fact that we are resting wholly on the Son of God.

'I am glorified in them' is the divine assessment of their life and service. It is the same as when He had said, 'they have kept thy word'. They had not always kept His word, nor had He always been glorified in them, but here is the general and divine assessment of the life and service of these men. To me, that is a precious thought.

'And now I am no more in the world, but these are in the world, and I come to thee. Holy Father, keep through thine own name those whom thou hast given me, that they may be one, as we are', v. 11

The Son of God was very much in the world when He said this, for in chapter 18 He goes forth over the brook Cedron. The right way to understand this prayer, then, is to see that though the Son was physically in the world He is, in spirit, in heaven.

One can feel the very throbbing of the heart of the Son of God when He said, 'but these are in the world, and I come to thee'. This links very much with chapter 13 verse 1. He was leaving the world but His heart was with these men so much that He wanted the Father to continue to do for them what He had done while He was with them.

When He speaks about Himself in the first section, verses 1 to 5, it is 'O Father'. When He speaks in respect of His own in this section it is 'Holy Father'. They are still in an evil world and they have to be kept. When He speaks in respect of the world, it is 'O righteous Father'. This last reference links to chapter 16 verse 10, where He says that the Holy Spirit would convict the world 'of righteousness, because I go to my Father'.

164

'Keep through' is really 'keep in'. He has already told the Father that He has manifested His name to them. He had kept them in the Father's name by His example and His teaching but now He asks the Father to keep them in the sanctuary of His own name, in the sanctuary of knowing Him as Father.

When someone is in the enjoyment of the fact of having a Father and, kneeling down, can meaningfully and worshipfully say, 'Father', that person is saved. To be able to do this when under great personal pressure, relief immediately sweeps over the soul. There is a sanctuary, a keeping power, in knowing God as Father. The appreciation of divine realities is the greatest preservation from the world's unrealities.

There are three references to oneness in this prayer, in verses 11, 21, and 22. In trying to understand these three expressions it is necessary to remember for whom the Lord is praying. In this verse, He is praying for the apostles, the disciples who were then with Him, as the next verse makes clear. This is, therefore, an apostolic, objective oneness, 'one, as we'. He thinks of them being one in name, object, purpose and harmony. Accordingly, it is not, 'one, as we are' but 'one, as we'. Also, the oneness for which He prays is not partial or transient.

It is, of course, impossible to think that any prayer of God's Son would ever remain unanswered. The prayer of this verse was wonderfully answered in those pentecostal days on the part of the apostles. Consider how this was fulfilled. In Acts chapter 1 verse 13, the names of the eleven apostles are given, the next verse stating that, 'These all continued with one accord in prayer and supplication, with the women'. They are praying with one accord; the Lord's prayer is being answered. In Acts chapter 2 verse 1, 'they were all with one accord in one place'; the Lord's prayer is being answered. In Acts chapter 2 verse 14, 'Peter, standing up with the eleven, lifted up his voice'. Later, in verses 41 and 42, they continued steadfastly in the teaching and fellowship of the apostles, all in accordance with the Lord's prayer that they may be one.

This prayer was for apostolic oneness and for that reason it was also objective, that they may be one in aim and in object. It was necessary

165

that this should be so because these men, who were listening to the Son of God praying, were to form the nucleus of the church. Also, it was to their fellowship that believers were received, and in that fellowship they continued.

The oneness of verse 21 is oneness in affection and love and refers to pentecostal union. The oneness of verse 22 is future and involves the whole church in a oneness in future glory. Undoubtedly there are principles in this section which, in the first instance, applied to the apostles but which are true for us now.

'While I was with them in the world, I kept them in thy name: those that thou gavest me I have kept, and none of them is lost, but the son of perdition; that the scripture might be fulfilled', v. 12

Here is a lovely statement, that those whom the Father has given to the Son have been kept and none will ever be lost. This verse makes it clear that Judas Iscariot was never given by the Father to the Son, but he was the son of perdition. He could not escape perdition.

He kept them in the sanctuary of 'the Father's name', keeping them in the enjoyment of the blessed relationship of knowing God as Father. He did this in two ways at least. He made known the Father's name by teaching, but He also kept them in the enjoyment of that relationship by His example, always living before them, revealing the Father.

There are two different words for 'keep' in this verse. The first, *tēreō*, has the idea of 'keeping one's eye upon' but the second, *phulassō*, is a little stronger, having the idea of 'guarding'. It is impossible, for any who have been given as a love gift by the Father to the Son, ever to be lost. He would never lose what the Father has given to Him, and keeps them to this end.

While He was with them in the world, none of them was lost. The one who was lost was, in fact, never saved; he was the son of perdition. 1 Corinthians chapter 1 verse 18 speaks of 'those' who are perishing and of 'us' who are being saved. Those who are perishing are going on to eternal perdition, whereas those who are being saved are going on to

166

ultimate salvation. Men and women who are without God in the world are perishing and will perish, ultimately to spend eternity without God. The words 'lost' and 'perdition' are really the same word. 'None perishes, but the son of perishing'.

This appellation does not just refer to Judas because, in 2 Thessalonians 2 verse 3, there is another reference. There are some who think that this is a name and that the reference is to Judas Iscariot. However, both Judas Iscariot and the man of sin are designated 'son of perdition'. The idea in the phrase is that they cannot escape perdition and are seen as the embodiment of sin. Some remarkable things are said about Judas. Satan put the thought into his heart, entered into him and took such possession of him that he could not be separated from Satan himself, as a demon.

Men might apostatize but God will never be defeated. He makes the wrath of man to praise Him. If Judas is an apostate, there was one who would make up the twelve in Acts chapter 1. If there is the man of sin, the antichrist, then there is the Christ Himself. God will not be defeated.

The reason why Judas was amongst the twelve was that the scripture might be fulfilled. The reference is to Psalm 41 verse 9. The Lord dealt with him on the ground of his profession until, in chapter 13, he made it quite patent that he was an apostate. It was not until then that the Lord said, 'That thou doest, do quickly'. A little while before that, the Lord had even washed his feet. Some people stumble at that but what is characteristic of the ways of God is that He will always take up a man on his profession until that profession might be proved to be false.

Spiritism is apostasy. The charismatic movement claims miracles, but we could not think that those who are involved are apostates. Remember, it is not what men claim by way of what they do, or experience, that is the acid test of everything; the acid test is, 'What saith the scripture?' In Matthew chapter 7 verse 22, the Lord Jesus speaks of those who will say that they have done things in His name. They are not content just to say 'Lord, Lord'. Those who profess most loudly as to their relationship to the Lord, and boast of what they are able to do, are always suspect. The man who is truly genuine is happy to go on quietly with the Lord. Of course, that is the kind of thing that is rare today.

God never engineers or manipulates anything, but, in His foreknowledge, stated in Psalm 41 what Judas would do. Judas was not chosen to do this, but he was chosen because he would do this.

'And now come I to thee; and these things I speak in the world, that they might have my joy fulfilled in themselves', v. 13

He has already spoken to them about His joy. 'These things have I spoken unto you, that my joy might remain in you, and that your joy might be full', 15. 11. He is there teaching them about the necessity of abiding in the Father's love and as they did this so His joy would be fulfilled in them. The simple thought in this verse, however, is that as He spoke in the world and as they listened, they learned something of the wonder of communion between the Son and the Father. The joy of which He speaks is the joy of communion with heaven and with the Father, the joy of an unclouded spirit. They hear the evidence of this as they listen to the Son of God praying. Therefore, He prays in their hearing for their spiritual enrichment, that they might have His joy fulfilled in themselves and enter into the joy of uninterrupted communion with the Father and with heaven.

'I have given them thy word; and the world hath hated them, because they are not of the world, even as I am not of the world', v. 14

If, in verse 13, there is His joy, in verse 14, there is the world's hatred.

The word of the Father that He had given them was the word that reveals the Father. The knowledge of God as Jehovah made a distinction between Jew and Gentile, but the knowledge of God as Father makes a distinction between the child of God and the world.

At the end of the prayer, He says, 'O righteous Father, the world hath not known thee'. In chapter 1 verse 10, 'He was in the world . . . and the world knew him not'. He came to the world and was with His own at the same time. In that the world knew Him not, there was ignorance, but in that His own received Him not, there was rejection. It is the ignorance of the world that is estranged from God. The Lord has already said, in chapter 16, that by reason of His presence with them the world's hatred was particularly directed against Him and that, to a large extent, He had preserved them from it but when He left them they would experience that hatred.

The context always determines what the word 'world' means. For instance, 'He was in the world . . . and the world knew him not', John 1. 10. He was in the world that His hands had made but the world of humanity knew Him not. 'Love not the world, neither the things that are in the world', 1 John 2. 15, does not refer to the physical world, or the world of humanity, but the world system that is estranged from God. That system is all around us, men and women content to dispense with God and live without Him. Indeed, the world lies unconcernedly in the lap of the wicked one. Thus, the world is seen in a threefold way.

We are not of the world. We have been chosen out of it as to our source, we are not of it as to our character and we are not of it as to our destiny. God has taken us out of the world so that though we are in it we are not of it. Praise God, the world is not our destiny; heaven is our home. We are glad to think that we are not of the world as to its condemnation but we should be equally glad that we are not of the world as to its character, the things that it loves and seeks. I believe that the unworldliness of God's people is something the devil is trying to destroy today. The world is creeping into our hearts, into our homes and into assemblies, and we are becoming more and more like the world out of which we have been taken. Where the devil has failed, down the years, in terms of violence, he has now succeeded in terms of corruption. The world still hates us: it has not changed.

When we think of the world politically, morally and ecclesiastically, Paul says, 'I [am crucified] unto the world', Gal. 6. 14. He has in view the religious world, but it is true of the world in all its aspects.

'I pray not that thou shouldest take them out of the world, but that thou shouldest keep them from the evil', v. 15

He does not want them to be taken out of the world, for the reason stated in verse 20. The Lord could have saved them and taken them out of the world, but they are left here as others are going to believe on Him through their word. In this the Lord makes it clear that He never intended that His children should live a monastic life in isolation from the world. They are to be in the world, though not of it, as a testimony to others so that they might believe.

This world is an evil world and at Calvary its evil was made patent when it condemned to crucifixion the Son of God from heaven. We are not promised exemption but we are promised protection, because He prayed, 'keep them from the evil'. The thought here is not of 'the evil one' but the evil of the world. In Matthew chapter 6 verse 13, in the prayer that the Lord taught His disciples, the reference is to the evil one, 'deliver us from the evil one' RV. It can be seen that this is the case as the prayer will have special significance in the day when the devil will be here on earth, in the time of Jacob's trouble.

It is the Father who keeps us from the evil, provided that we are cast upon Him. We cannot do this for ourselves. The greatest help in being kept from evil is to live in touch with the Father, recognizing our own weakness. Left to ourselves we will succumb to the evil, but the Father will keep us from it. I heard MR. FRANK KNOX say several times that he started each day with the words of Psalm 16 verse 1, 'Preserve me, O God: for in thee do I put my trust'. We are 'kept by the power of God', which is always available to faith, 1 Pet. 1. 5.

'They are not of the world, even as I am not of the world', v. 16

The repetition of this truth shows how important it is. Since we are not of the world it is not for the child of God to participate in its affairs.

'Sanctify them through thy truth: thy word is truth', v. 17

The word 'sanctify' can easily be understood. To purify means to make pure; to justify means to make just or righteous; to sanctify means to be set apart and made holy.

There is a sense in which the moment I put my trust in Christ I was sanctified and made holy in His sight. This is a sanctification that cannot be improved upon, that is not progressive, and which means that the moment that I trusted Christ I was fit for heaven. That is what might be termed positional sanctification. In 1 Corinthians chapter 1 verse 2, we read of those who are 'sanctified in Christ Jesus, called to be saints'. This happens immediately upon believing in Christ. In 1 Corinthians chapter 6 verse 11, the apostle speaks of the Corinthians as having been washed, sanctified and justified 'in the name of the Lord Jesus, and by the Spirit of our God'. When a person puts trust in Christ, he is washed in God's sight, justified in God's sight and sanctified in God's sight. Hebrews chapter 10 verse 10 says, 'By the which will we are sanctified through the offering of the body of Jesus Christ once for all'. Jesus offered His body to accomplish the will of God, which was our sanctification, our being set apart in His sight. The moment we put our trust in Christ that was true. This is not progressive but positional; it cannot be improved upon.

There is also a practical sanctification, a working out in the life of positional sanctification. Here, our Lord prays, 'Sanctify them through thy truth: thy word is truth'. It is the Father, through the word, who produces in us practical sanctification. It is not just by the word of 'God' but the word of 'truth'; 'thy word is truth'. This is the truth of God forming me and fashioning me, building me up spiritually and preserving me from the evil influences of the world.

There is, therefore, everything in the word of God to help the Christian to live a sanctified life. However, it is not just reading, knowing, preaching or teaching the word that leads to practical sanctification. It is only as we allow the word to judge, wound, expose and cleanse us that we are sanctified. In reading the word, we must listen to God speaking to our hearts, telling us where we have failed Him, exposing

171

to us the wrongs in our life and those things that are unworthy which hinder our spiritual progress. There can be a serious danger of just reading the word and acquiring personal knowledge to be able to preach and teach but our personal sanctification is more important than that.

In verse 19, it is not so much being sanctified 'through the truth' but 'in truth' or being 'sanctified truly'. This is practical sanctification. Peter says, 'Be ye holy; for I am holy', 1 Pet. 1. 16. We are called upon to be holy because the God who has sanctified us is holy. Paul says, 'let us cleanse ourselves from all filthiness of the flesh and spirit, perfecting holiness in the fear of God', 2 Cor. 7. 1. We cannot perfect what we are in Christ but we can perfect practical holiness in the fear of God. The teaching of 1 John chapter 3 verse 3 is that he who has his hope set on Christ 'purifieth himself, even as he [Christ] is pure'. If my eye is heavenward, looking for the coming of the pure one, it will have a sanctifying and purifying effect upon me. There are other aspects of the truth of sanctification that we cannot touch on now.

'As thou hast sent me into the world, even so have I also sent them into the world', v. 18

This is an amazing statement. It is a new commission. Hitherto, the commission in Matthew chapter 10, Luke chapter 9 and Mark chapter 6 was to go to the lost sheep of the house of Israel, and was given by the Lord in the days of His flesh. Here, however, the Lord is viewed from the standpoint of the work being finished and His being on resurrection ground. This is a unique commission and is given again in chapter 20 verse 21. The best that could be said of servants in the Old Testament is what was said of John the Baptist, that he was 'a man sent from God' but now we are sent by the Son, John chapter 17, and by the risen Lord, chapter 20.

There are two words translated to 'send'. There is an official sending, *apostellō*, which is the word here, of the apostles. In John chapter 20 verse 21, it is not official, for it is not there confined to the apostles as there were more than the apostles present in the upper room. There, the word used is *pempō*. All are sent, therefore, though strictly it has in view only the apostles in this verse.

'And for their sakes I sanctify myself, that they also might be sanctified through the truth', v. 19

The thought is not so much one of being sanctified 'through the truth' but sanctified 'in truth', or 'truly'.

Now, the Lord sanctifies Himself. Obviously, our Lord did not need to be set apart or made holy; moral sanctification was never necessary on the part of our Lord for He is pure. This is not, therefore, moral sanctification but physical sanctification. It is not being sanctified from one state to another, from being unholy to becoming holy, but being set apart from one place to another. He is speaking of going back to heaven for the sake of His own, that they might be sanctified truly. He has set Himself apart in heaven that we might find in Him an object there to fill and to satisfy the heart. He has set Himself apart in heaven that we might truly be set apart for Him on earth. These are very important matters.

Consecration is an Old Testament word. The corresponding thought in the New Testament is 'to be perfected'. The natural meaning of consecration is 'the filling of the hands'. When the priest had his hands filled by Moses with the things which speak of Christ, he was perfected in the sight of God. Our consecration is not so much when our hands are filled but when our heart is full of Christ. The Lord Jesus said in Mark chapter 7 verses 21 to 23, 'For from within, out of the heart of men, proceed evil thoughts, adulteries, fornications, murders, thefts, covetousness, wickedness, deceit, lasciviousness, an evil eye, blasphemy, pride, foolishness: all these evil things come from within, and defile the man'. The evil things that defile us start not with the body but in the heart. However, we have one who is set apart in heaven to occupy, to fill, and to satisfy the heart. If He fills the heart then those evil things that commence in the heart are expunged and cast out. This is true practical sanctification.

In Genesis chapter 3 verse 6, sin entered body, soul and spirit. Eve saw that the tree was 'good for food', relating to the body, 'pleasant to the eyes', relating to the soul, and 'desired to make one wise', relating to the spirit. Sin could only enter that way for man was innocent. It was because His heart was right that sin needed to come from the outside into the body, soul and spirit. Sanctification for the believer, however, is not body, soul and spirit but is from the inside. 1 Thessalonians chapter 5 verse 23 says, 'And the very God of peace sanctify you wholly; and I pray God your whole spirit and soul and body be preserved blameless unto the coming of our Lord Jesus Christ'. Thus, practical sanctification does not begin in the body but in the spirit, the inner man.

The reason why so many of us fail in the matter of practical sanctification is that we begin on the outside, with the body, but we must begin on the inside. When He fills the heart then we become truly sanctified. Colossians chapter 3 teaches us that we shall never be able to mortify the members which are upon the earth if we have not first of all set the mind on things above, in heaven.

What an object we have in heaven! The Son of God set Himself apart there for us so that, as our hearts are filled with Him, we become truly sanctified. 2 Corinthians chapter 3 verse 18 says, 'But we all, with open face beholding as in a glass the glory of the Lord, are changed into the same image from glory to glory, even as by the Spirit of the Lord'. Christendom puts its monks and nuns behind the walls of large convents and monasteries, but this does not produce sanctified lives. Walls might shut in the body but they can never shut out the thoughts and evil desires. Practical sanctification is that which deals with the thought life; He is set apart in heaven and as we think on and are occupied with Him in heaven, Christ filling the heart, so we shall be sanctified truly on the earth.

For true practical sanctification, every thought must be brought into captivity. The Lord Jesus said, 'if therefore thine eye be single, thy whole body shall be full of light', Matt. 6. 22. This means that if we have a single eye for Him the evil thoughts are excluded. We are not exempt from them but we deal with them at their inception.

174

This has to do with the ministry of the Spirit. The Spirit occupies our thoughts with the man who is set apart in heaven for us.

Believers – oneness, vv. 20-26

'Neither pray I for these alone, but for them also which shall believe on me through their word', v. 20

In verses 20 to 26, He speaks to the Father about those who would believe on Him through the testimony of those who were then with Him. Now He prays for the pentecostal saints, the infant church.

In chapter 15 verse 27, He said to these same disciples, 'And ye also shall bear witness, because ye have been with me from the beginning'. There is no mention there of the intention in the witness they would bear or its anticipated results. The result would, in fact, be that there would be those who would believe on Him through their word. In verse 14, He had told them that the world had hated them and would hate them but despite this the message had to be preached. God was interested in the salvation of people in the world and they would believe on Him through their word.

He did not pray in verse 15 that they would be taken out of the world, in view of the fact that that there would be those who would believe on Him through their word. His people are left in the world, therefore, that others might believe on Him through their word. He had already said, 'I have given them thy word', and now it is a matter of His own giving the word to the world. The word is not just the same as He received from the Father but, more generally, the word of truth.

The Lord here states, as He did in other places, that the means by which God reaches men with His salvation is through the word of His disciples, or His servants. This is a matter which we would do well to remember. The means has never changed from New Testament times. Romans chapter 10 verses 14 and 15 gives the divine order, which is that the servant is sent, he preaches so that people might hear and that having heard they might believe, call upon the Lord and be saved. As it was then, so it must be today.

The verse speaks of the word. The word used has no thought of 'heralding' but is simply a statement of the word of truth. In Matthew chapter 13 verse 19, the seed is the word, but in 1 Peter chapter 1 verse 23 it is not the seed of the field but the incorruptible seed of the Spirit by the word.

'That they all may be one; as thou, Father, art in me, and I in thee, that they also may be one in us: that the world may believe that thou hast sent me', v. 21

His prayer for those who would believe through the apostles' word was that they might be 'one in us'. This is the second reference of three to oneness. In verse 11, He was praying particularly for the apostles and we have noted how this was fulfilled in the book of Acts. This was an objective oneness: one in aim, one in object, one in desire. This was so necessary because the apostles, being the nucleus of the church, were the basis of Christianity. Now, however, He refers not just to the apostles but to those who would believe on Him through the word of the apostles.

If 'one, as we' is objective in verse 11, 'one in us' is subjective. This is not a oneness of life or oneness in church order, nor is it a reference to the one body but a subjective, heavenly oneness in terms of love and affection. He prays that as the Father is in the Son's love and affection, and the Son is in the Father's love and affection, so they also might be one in the Father and Son's love and affection. It is therefore a subjective oneness, a oneness in divine love and affection.

It is wonderful to think that this being one in the Father and the Son in terms of divine love and affection was enjoyed by those early saints. Whereas they were formerly hateful and hating one another, Titus 3. 3, there was now this oneness in love and affection.

It had in view 'that the world may believe that thou hast sent me'. It is impossible to think of a prayer of God's Son remaining unanswered. In

176

Acts chapters 1 and 2, we see that the prayer of verse 11 is answered in respect of apostolic oneness, but we also see how that the prayer of this verse is fulfilled. Acts chapter 2 verses 44 and 45 say, 'And all that believed were together, and had all things common; and sold their possessions and goods, and parted them to all men, as every man had need'. Then, in chapter 4 verse 23, when Peter and John had been in prison and there had been an attempt to intimidate them, 'they went to their own company'. In the next verse, the disciples 'lifted up their voice to God with one accord' and 'great grace was upon them all', v. 33. Remarkable oneness of love and affection marked the early saints and so here it is a testimony not by preaching, as in verse 20, but a testimony of heavenly oneness in love and affection.

Particularly in those pentecostal days, not long after Jesus was condemned, rejected and crucified, when people saw a company in whom was manifested divine love and affection, they would say that the one who was crucified must have been the one whom the Father sent. Although this was pentecostal and subjective, and also transient, yet there is an abiding principle that if the world round about us sees in us oneness in divine love and affection they will have to say that it is true that the Father sent the Son.

In verse 20, it speaks of those who 'shall believe on me through their word'. This is believing 'on' Him, but in verse 21 it is not that the world may believe on Him but 'that the world may believe that thou hast sent me'. In verse 20, it is saving faith, believing on Him. In verse 21, however, it is not necessarily saving faith because it is not believing 'on him' but believing a fact, that the Father sent the Son.

'And the glory which thou gavest me I have given them; that they may be one, even as we are one', v. 22

This is evidently a glory that the Son can communicate. 'The glory which thou gavest me I have given them'. This cannot be His divine, essential glory, which is incommunicable, but the acquired glory referred to in verse 1, where He prayed, 'glorify thy Son, that thy Son also may glorify thee'. It is the glory that the Father has now given the Son in answer to what the Son was here, and He has shared it with us.

There are different aspects to the Son's glory. In John chapter 11 verse 4, it says, 'This sickness is not unto death, but for the glory of God, that the Son of God might be glorified thereby'. This was the glorification of the Son of God in His power in resurrection, by raising a man from the dead. In Romans chapter 1 verse 4, it says that He was 'declared to be the Son of God with power, according to the spirit of holiness', by the resurrection of dead ones. If, in John chapter 11, it is the glorification of the Son of God, in Romans chapter 1 it is the glorification of the Son of man, as it is in John chapter 13 verse 31 where the Son of man was glorified in that He submitted Himself to death. In Hebrews chapter 5, He has a priestly glory. The passage is teaching that the Old Testament priesthood was a priesthood that not just any man could assume; the priests had to be called and it was to an honour that they did not deserve. In contrast, Christ's priesthood is not an honour that He does not deserve but a glory that has been added.

The glory has not yet been given to us, despite the employment of the past tense. As far as divine persons are concerned, this is something as good as accomplished. This is the Son speaking to the Father, and when divine persons are addressing each other it is never a matter of 'when' but a matter of 'what'. Time does not come into it. In the divine reckoning, we are foreknown, predestinated, called, justified and already glorified. In the divine reckoning, as the Son speaks to the Father, we have already been given this glory, but the realization of it for us is yet future.

It is not now 'that they may be one, as we', v. 11, or 'one in us', v. 21, but 'that they may be one, even as we are one'. This refers to the whole church. They would be one as the Father and the Son are one in terms of glory. 'I in them, and thou in me, that they may be made perfect in one', v. 23. This is the Son glorified in the saints and the Father glorified in the Son. Here, it is to do with being perfected into oneness of glory, a oneness in manifested glory.

The Son has already said, 'I have glorified thee on the earth', v. 4. In verse 1, He tells the Father that He intends to continue to glorify Him in heaven as He has done on earth. He now tells the Father that he does not intend to retain this acquired glory for Himself but will share it with others. He is glorified in heaven where He glorifies the Father, and, in the future, He is going to share that glory with us. It is easy to speak about these things and to lose the impact of them. Think of the Son sharing His glory with us!

In verse 24, when the Son expresses the desire of His heart 'that they may behold my glory', He speaks of a glory that we cannot share but which we are going to behold, His own incommunicable glory.

'I in them, and thou in me, that they may be made perfect in one; and that the world may know that thou hast sent me, and hast loved them, as thou hast loved me', v. 23

Oneness in glory is explained in the expression, 'I in them, and thou in me'. When He shares His glory, the result is that He, the Son, will be glorified in the saints, and the Father will be glorified in the Son, that they may be perfected into one. This will be realized at our Saviour's appearing. Colossians chapter 3 verses 3 and 4 speak of our life being 'hid with Christ in God' but that 'When Christ, who is our life shall appear, then shall ye also appear with him in glory'. Appearing in glory with Him means that He has shared His glory with us. In 2 Thessalonians chapter 1 verse 10, when He comes, He will 'be glorified in his saints' and 'admired in all them that believe'. It is not here that He will be glorified 'by' His saints but 'in' them. This will happen as He shares His glory with us. When the world sees us sharing with the Son the glory that the Father has given to Him, the Son will be glorified in us.

> The heavens shall glow with splendour,
> But brighter far than they,
> The saints shall shine in glory,
> As Christ shall them array.
> The beauty of the Saviour
> Shall dazzle every eye,
> In the crowning day that's coming
> By-and-by.
>
> [DANIEL W. WHITTLE]

There is a twofold aspect to our Lord's appearing and both are noted in 2 Thessalonians chapter 1. Not only will the Lord come 'to be glorified in his saints', v. 10, but, in verses 7 and 8, He is to be 'revealed from heaven with his mighty angels, in flaming fire taking vengeance on them that know not God, and that obey not the gospel of our Lord Jesus Christ'. In Revelation chapter 19 verse 11, He comes forth from heaven on a white horse, in judgement making war. In Revelation chapter 21, from verse 10 onwards, He is appearing in glory with the saints, the holy city Jerusalem, having, and radiating, the glory of God. This is the appearing in glory, the same event from another standpoint, He appears, therefore both in judgement and in glory.

In verse 21 it is 'that the world may believe' but here it is 'that the world may know'. It is not 'that the world may believe', when He shares this glory with us for it will be too late then for the world to believe. It is 'that the world may know' in terms of recognizing two facts, which are that the Father sent the Son and that the Father loved us as He had loved the Son. Thus, when we appear in glory with the Saviour the world will recognize that the one to whom it gave a cross was the one whom the Father sent, and that those they hated, v. 14, are those whom the Father loved.

Many have recurring doubts as to whether they are saved or not. So many of us only think that salvation is sins forgiven, being saved from hell and being brought to heaven, but there is far more to salvation than that. The Father loves us as He loves His Son. If we could enter experientially into this truth then we would not have such recurring doubts. Anything else would not become the God that we love. God, who has upon His heart our highest good and our highest bliss, has not only marked us out to be like His Son in the future but He loves us now as He loves His own Son. This is something that the world is going to recognize when we appear in glory with our Saviour.

The world shall recognize these things by sight which have hitherto been unrevealed. In Luke chapter 9 verse 26, we read about 'when he shall come in his own glory, and in his Father's, and of the holy angels'. That is a tremendous thing but here we learn something in addition, that He will share His own glory with us.

Notice it is 'that they may be made perfect in one'. The Father will see to it that what was established in grace in verse 21 will be perfected in glory, verse 23.

'Father, I will that they also, whom thou hast given me, be with me where I am; that they may behold my glory, which thou hast given me: for thou lovedst me before the foundation of the world', v. 24

In verse 9, He had said, 'I pray', or 'I demand', but this is something very intimate, 'Father, I will'. It is His desire based on relationship with the Father and He seems to say, 'I am thy Son, and this is my desire'.

In the garden of Gethsemane, He is prostrate on the earth sweating, weeping and in agony. He says, 'not as I will'. Here, however, His eyes are lifted up into heaven and He is thinking not only of the glory but of our being with Him to behold it. He does not now say, 'not as I will' but 'Father, I will'. In Gethsemane He is contemplating enduring on the cross for us the hell that our sins so richly deserved, and He says, 'not as I will'. Now, however, He is thinking of the heaven that we could never have deserved, and He says, 'Father, I will'.

We have seen that we are able to watch the movements of the Son in this prayer. 'I have glorified thee on the earth', v. 4; 'I am no more in the world', v. 11; 'I come to thee', v. 11. Now He is with the Father, desiring that they should be with Him. He speaks of them being with Him, 'where I am', not where He was when He prayed, or where He was on the cross, or even where He was as a risen man. Now He is, in spirit, at God's right hand and He wills that we should be with Him where He is.

Some render it, 'Father, I will that that which thou hast given me be with me where I am'. 'That which' would simply refer to the church as a body rather than to each of them individually being the Father's love gift to the Son.

Heaven is heaven because it is just to be 'with me'. To the dying thief He said, 'To day shalt thou be with me', Luke. 23. 43. He did not say, 'To day shalt thou be in paradise', but 'To day shalt thou be with me in paradise'. In Philippians chapter 1 verse 23, the apostle speaks of

181

having a desire to depart, not to be 'in heaven' but 'with Christ'. Again, 2 Corinthians chapter 5 verse 8 speaks of being 'absent from the body' and 'present', or at home, not 'in heaven' but 'with the Lord'. That is heaven! There is something more important than the golden street. Heaven is to be with Him and it is His desire to have us there.

We have seen, in verse 22, that He is going to share His glory with us and, therefore, we shall be like Him, but this is something in advance of this. John chapters 14 and 17 have to be taken together. In chapter 14 verse 3, He says, 'And if I go and prepare a place for you, I will come again, and receive you unto myself; that where I am, there ye may be also'. In chapter 17, however, we learn not just a statement of a fact but that it is the desire of His heart for us to be with Him. Thus, there are three things here, to be like Him, to be with Him, and to behold His glory.

'My glory' is stronger than 'the glory which thou gavest me', v. 22. Here it is His own divine and essential glory. Certainly, it says 'my glory, which thou hast given me' but this links with verse 5, where He has resumed the position that is proper to His own divine and essential glory. This is confirmed by the expression, 'for thou lovedst me before the foundation of the world'. He goes away beyond time and creation here and so it is a glory that He cannot share. However, we shall behold this glory. It is a man in Godhood glory, occupying a position that belongs exclusively to deity, sharing all the glory of deity, yet still in a body that bears the marks of Calvary. This is the Ark of shittim wood overlaid within and without with gold. What a tremendous thought! That is 'my glory', a glory that He cannot share; it is something that the world will never see but that we are going to behold. The glory that He shares is connected with His appearing and kingdom, as we have already seen, but 'my glory' is connected with the Father's house.

This verse confirms His eternal Sonship especially, establishing a Father's love toward the Son before the foundation of the world.

This is the last reference in the prayer to those whom the Father has given to the Son. There are seven gifts of the Father to the Son in this prayer. One of these He mentions seven times. The gifts are: authority,

v. 2; the work, v. 4; all things, v. 7; the words, v. 8; the glory, v. 22; my glory, v. 24. The seventh gift, which He mentions seven times, is those whom the Father has given Him. Of all the things that the Father has given to the Son we are greater than anything else.

'O righteous Father, the world hath not known thee: but I have known thee, and these have known that thou hast sent me', v. 25

Here, there is the difference between the Son and the world and between the disciple and the world. The world does not know the Father but the Son knows the Father. The disciples have known, in contrast to the world, that the Father sent the Son.

In verses 25 and 26, there is the grand climax to the prayer in which the Son addresses the Father as 'righteous Father'. He addresses Him as 'Holy Father' in connection with its evil, and 'righteous Father' in connection with its ignorance of the Father.

He addresses the Father as 'righteous Father' because in chapter 16 verse 8 He said that the Comforter would convict 'the world of sin, and of righteousness, and of judgement'. He would convict the world 'of righteousness, because I go to my Father', v. 10. He says this for the simple reason that He was here a holy, flawless man, but the religious and political worlds condemned Him. He could go nowhere else but to the Father. The thought in 'O righteous Father' is that the Son would go to the Father because there is no righteousness down here. He was condemned in this world because it was ignorant of the Father and there was only one place to which He could go.

'And I have declared unto them thy name, and will declare it: that the love wherewith thou hast loved me may be in them, and I in them', v. 26

There is a beautiful thought with which the prayer concludes. We have the Father's love toward the Son in us and the Son Himself in us. The Son will continue to do what He has been doing, namely declaring the Father's name, making the Father known to us, so that the Father's love to Him when He was down here as man might be in His own. 'And I in

183

them' means that He will be in them as the means of enjoying the Father's love toward us.

In Psalm 22 verse 22 and Hebrews chapter 2 verse 12, He says, 'I will declare thy name unto my brethren'. He manifested the Father's name to them in His life and declared it to them in His resurrection. He did this when He said to Mary to go to His brethren and say, 'I ascend unto my Father', John 20. 17.